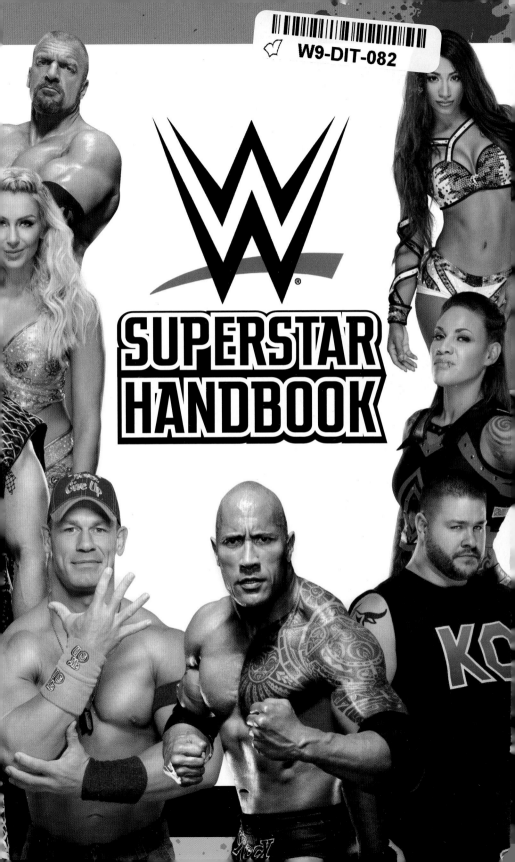

SUPERSTAR HANDBOOK

ADAM COLE

Since his debut in 2017, Adam Cole has dominated NXT. He became the longest-reigning NXT Champion, holding the gold for over a year. And that's Undisputed, "Bay Bay!"

HEIGHT: 6ft (1.83m)
WEIGHT: 210lbs (95kg)
HOMETOWN: Panama City, Florida
SIGNATURE MOVE: Panama Sunrise
RIVALS: Velveteen Dream, Johnny Gargano

AKIRA TOZAWA

Known for his stiff kicks and hard-hitting suplexes, Akira Tozawa is a staple of WWE's Cruiserweight Division. He now has his sights set on the NXT Cruiserweight Championship.

HEIGHT: 5ft 7in (1.70m)
WEIGHT: 156lbs (71kg)
HOMETOWN: Kobe, Japan
SIGNATURE MOVE: Snap German Suplex
RIVALS: The Brian Kendrick

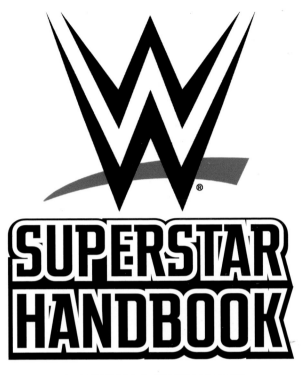

SUPERSTAR HANDBOOK

WRITTEN BY JAKE BLACK

"The Phenomenal One" AJ Styles has repeatedly demonstrated his talents in the ring, capturing the WWE Championship less than a year after his 2016 debut.

HEIGHT: 5ft 11in (1.80m)
WEIGHT: 218lbs (99kg)
HOMETOWN: Gainesville, Georgia
SIGNATURE MOVE: Phenomenal Forearm, Styles Clash
RIVALS: John Cena, Kevin Owens

ALBERT

A star of the Attitude Era, Albert left WWE to compete in Japan before returning to battle Superstars like John Cena. He is now head coach at the WWE Performance Center.

HEIGHT: 6ft 7in (2.01m)
WEIGHT: 331lbs (150kg)
HOMETOWN: Boston, Massachusetts
SIGNATURE MOVE: Cannonball
RIVALS: Undertaker, John Cena

ALEISTER BLACK

This mysterious and intimidating Dutchman has destroyed countless opponents, demonstrating skills that have made him a top contender for the WWE Championship.

HEIGHT: 6ft (1.83m)
WEIGHT: 215lbs (98kg)
HOMETOWN: Amsterdam, The Netherlands
SIGNATURE MOVE: Black Mass
RIVALS: Seth Rollins, Murphy

ALEXA BLISS

Competitive and determined, Alexa Bliss rules the WWE Women's Division. She was the first Superstar to win both the *RAW* and *SmackDown* Women's Championships.

HEIGHT: 5ft 1in (1.55m)
HOMETOWN: Columbus, Ohio
SIGNATURE MOVE: Twisted Bliss
RIVALS: Becky Lynch, Bayley

ALEXANDER WOLFE

Originally a key member of the SAnitY stable, Alexander Wolfe later joined Imperium in his native Europe. He won championship gold in both the UK and US versions of NXT.

HEIGHT: 6ft 1in (1.85m)
WEIGHT: 245lbs (111kg)
HOMETOWN: Dresden, Germany
SIGNATURE MOVE: Death Valley Driver
RIVALS: Undisputed ERA, British Strong Style

ALICIA TAYLOR

Before bringing her talents to NXT as a backstage interviewer, Alicia Taylor was a rock 'n' roll drummer, touring the world with some of the biggest acts in music.

HOMETOWN: Saginaw, Michigan

ALIYAH

A sports-entertainment fan since childhood, Aliyah began her in-ring career in NXT, targeting Chinese standout Xia Li. Aliyah now has her eyes on the NXT Women's Title.

HEIGHT: 5ft 3in (1.60m)
HOMETOWN: Toronto, Canada
SIGNATURE MOVE: Arabian Night
RIVALS: Xia Li, Io Shirai

ALUNDRA BLAYZE

Alundra Blayze revitalized the Women's Division in the mid-1990s. She held the Women's Championship for years, earning legendary status and a spot in the WWE Hall of Fame.

HEIGHT: 5ft 10in (1.78m)
HOMETOWN: Tampa, Florida
SIGNATURE MOVE: Bridging German Suplex
RIVALS: Wendi Richter, Bull Nakano

AMIR JORDAN

"The Bhangra Bad Boy" thrills the NXT UK Universe with his unique combination of aerial maneuvers and technical mat wrestling. His future is sure to be lined with championship gold.

HEIGHT: 5ft 11in (1.80m)
WEIGHT: 185lbs (84kg)
HOMETOWN: Dewsbury, England
SIGNATURE MOVE: Swanton Bomb
RIVALS: James Drake, Zack Gibson

ANDRÉ THE GIANT

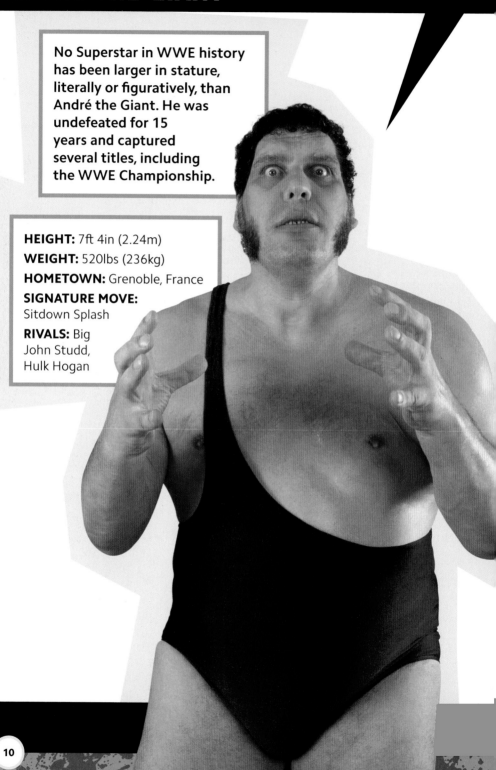

No Superstar in WWE history has been larger in stature, literally or figuratively, than André the Giant. He was undefeated for 15 years and captured several titles, including the WWE Championship.

HEIGHT: 7ft 4in (2.24m)
WEIGHT: 520lbs (236kg)
HOMETOWN: Grenoble, France
SIGNATURE MOVE: Sitdown Splash
RIVALS: Big John Studd, Hulk Hogan

ANDRADE

After becoming a major star in Mexico, Andrade brought his unique talents to WWE. He used his fast-paced aerial style to win the NXT Title and WWE United States Championship.

HEIGHT: 5ft 9in (1.75m)
WEIGHT: 210lbs (95kg)
HOMETOWN: Gómez Palacio, Mexico
SIGNATURE MOVE: Hammerlock DDT
RIVALS: Tye Dillinger, Cedric Alexander

ANGEL GARZA

A third-generation competitor, Angel Garza's in-ring career began at age 15. He joined NXT in 2019 and won the NXT Cruiserweight Championship before moving to *RAW*.

HEIGHT: 5ft 9in (1.75m)
WEIGHT: 207lbs (94kg)
HOMETOWN: Monterrey, Mexico
SIGNATURE MOVE: The Wing Clipper
RIVALS: Drew McIntyre, Rey Mysterio

REZAR

AKAM

The AOP barreled onto the scene in NXT, winning the Dusty Rhodes Tag Team Classic and the NXT Tag Team Championship. Now on *RAW*, they're the very definition of dominance.

AKA: The Authors of Pain
COMBINED WEIGHT: 620lbs (281kg)
SIGNATURE MOVE: The Last Chapter
RIVALS: American Alpha, #DIY

APOLLO CREWS

Named after an all-powerful Greek god, Apollo Crews brings maximum devastation to his WWE opponents. He is one of the physically strongest Superstars in all of WWE.

HEIGHT: 6ft 1in (1.85m)
WEIGHT: 240lbs (109kg)
HOMETOWN: Stone Mountain, Georgia
SIGNATURE MOVE: Standing Moonsault
RIVALS: Heath Slater, Dolph Ziggler

ARIYA DAIVARI

With an unmatched aggressive streak, Ariya Daivari has built an intimidating reputation as part of the Cruiserweight Division. Nicknamed "The Persian Lion," he roars in and out of the ring.

HEIGHT: 5ft 10in (1.78m)
WEIGHT: 190lbs (86kg)
HOMETOWN: Minneapolis, Minnesota
SIGNATURE MOVE: Frog Splash
RIVALS: Gentleman Jack Gallagher

ARTURO RUAS

A fighter's fighter, Arturo Ruas learned a variety of combat styles in his native Brazil, including Jiu-Jitsu and capoeira. He brought them to NXT, and he is determined to show them off.

HEIGHT: 6ft 2in (1.88m)
WEIGHT: 220lbs (100kg)
HOMETOWN: Rio De Janeiro, Brazil
SIGNATURE MOVE: Jiu-Jitsu Kick
RIVALS: Street Profits

ASHTON SMITH

Known for his exciting aerial arsenal, Ashton Smith is part of WWE's European brand. He uses his hard-hitting in-ring style to climb the ladder in search of championship gold.

HEIGHT: 5ft 8in (1.73m)
WEIGHT: 206lbs (93kg)
HOMETOWN: Manchester, England
SIGNATURE MOVE: Inverted DDT
RIVALS: Imperium

ASUKA

Dominating WWE since 2015, Asuka has destroyed every woman she's competed against and has held the NXT, *SmackDown*, *RAW*, and Women's Tag Team Titles.

HEIGHT: 5ft 3in (1.60m)
HOMETOWN: Osaka, Japan
SIGNATURE MOVE: Asuka Lock
RIVALS: Bayley, Ember Moon

AUSTIN THEORY

After joining NXT in 2019, Austin Theory was quickly recruited by Zelina Vega to join her faction on *RAW*. He was later kicked out and became Seth Rollins' disciple.

HEIGHT: 6ft 1in (1.85m)
WEIGHT: 220lbs (100kg)
HOMETOWN: Atlanta, Georgia
SIGNATURE MOVE: Moonsault
RIVALS: Andrade, Angel Garza

BAM BAM BIGELOW

A powerful giant who moved like a cruiserweight, Bam Bam Bigelow used his size and agility to win singles titles in ECW and WCW, and the WCW Tag Team Championship twice.

HEIGHT: 6ft 4in (1.93m)
WEIGHT: 390lbs (177kg)
HOMETOWN: Asbury Park, New Jersey
SIGNATURE MOVE: Greetings From Asbury Park
RIVALS: Goldberg, Tatanka

Nicknamed "The Animal," Batista is as strong as an ox and as vicious as a wolverine. He has devoured the best Superstars in WWE and captured six WWE World Titles.

NAMES: 6ft 6in (1.98m)
WEIGHT: 290lbs (132kg)
HOMETOWN: Washington, D.C.
SIGNATURE MOVE: Batista Bomb
RIVALS: John Cena, Triple H

BAYLEY

Bayley shed her former happy-go-lucky "hugger" image in favor of a more intense, aggressive attitude. She now battles all challengers in her mission to prove she's the best.

HEIGHT: 5ft 6in (1.68m)
HOMETOWN: San Jose, California
SIGNATURE MOVE:
Bayley-to-Belly Suplex
RIVALS: Sasha Banks, Alexa Bliss

BETH PHOENIX

Known as "The Glamazon," Beth Phoenix captured several championships in her time in WWE. Inducted into the WWE Hall of Fame in 2017, she is now a commentator for NXT.

HEIGHT: 5ft 7in (1.70m)
HOMETOWN: Buffalo, New York
SIGNATURE MOVE: The Glam Slam
RIVALS: Mickie James, Candice Michelle

Becky Lynch set out to make WWE history, and she did. She won the first-ever all-women main event at *WrestleMania 35*, capturing both the *RAW* and *SmackDown* Women's Championships.

HEIGHT:
5ft 6in (1.68m)

HOMETOWN:
Dublin, Ireland

SIGNATURE MOVE:
Dis-Arm-Her

RIVALS: Charlotte Flair, Alexa Bliss

BIANCA BELAIR

Bianca Belair calls herself "The EST of WWE" because she believes she's the fastest, strongest, and all-around best Superstar. She first competed in NXT before moving to *RAW*.

HEIGHT: 5ft 7in (1.70m)
HOMETOWN: Knoxville, Tennessee
SIGNATURE MOVE:
K.O.D. (Kiss of Death)
RIVALS: Rhea Ripley, Shayna Baszler

BIG BOSS MAN

A former prison guard, the Big Boss Man always made sure his opponents served hard time. He eventually left the ring to become Mr. McMahon's private security officer.

HEIGHT: 6ft 7in (2.01m)
WEIGHT: 330lbs (150kg)
HOMETOWN: Cobb County, Georgia
SIGNATURE MOVE: Boss Man Slam
RIVALS: "Ravishing" Rick Rude, Big Show

BIG E

An NXT and Intercontinental Champion, Big E has proved himself to be a powerful Superstar. As one of The New Day tag team, he has discovered even more power in positivity.

HEIGHT: 5ft 11in (1.80m)
WEIGHT: 285lbs (129kg)
HOMETOWN: Tampa, Florida
SIGNATURE MOVE: Big Ending
RIVALS: The Usos,
The Miz and John Morrison

BIG JOHN STUDD

Part of an elite group of giants in WWE, Big John Studd aimed to prove he was the best of them. His rivalry with the biggest, André the Giant, defined his career.

HEIGHT: 6ft 10in (2.08m)
WEIGHT: 364lbs (165kg)
HOMETOWN: Los Angeles, California
SIGNATURE MOVE: Reverse Bear Hug
RIVALS: André the Giant

BIG SHOW

For decades, Big Show has made his massive presence known in WWE, winning multiple titles. The list of opponents he has slain is a virtual who's who of sports-entertainment royalty.

HEIGHT: 7ft (2.13m)
WEIGHT: 383lbs (174kg)
HOMETOWN: Tampa, Florida
SIGNATURE MOVE: Chokeslam
RIVALS: Undertaker, Kane

BILLY GUNN

A talented in-ring competitor, Billy Gunn's cocky attitude drew both the ire and love of the WWE Universe. He is best known as one half of the New Age Outlaws tag team.

HEIGHT: 6ft 4in (1.93m)
WEIGHT: 260lbs (118kg)
HOMETOWN: Orlando, Florida
SIGNATURE MOVE: Famouser
RIVALS: The Shield, Jamie Noble

BOA

After making a name for himself as a martial artist in China, Boa's lightning-quick skills caught the attention of NXT talent scouts. He came to the brand following a grueling four-day tryout in 2016.

HEIGHT: 6ft 4in (1.93m)
WEIGHT: 225lbs (102kg)
HOMETOWN: Beijing, China
SIGNATURE MOVE: Muay Thai Strike
RIVALS: Kona Reeves, Marcel Barthel

BO DALLAS

All you have to do is "Bo-lieve!" At least, that's what Bo Dallas says. His absolute confidence in himself is unparalleled, and it led him to win the *RAW* Tag Team Championship.

HEIGHT: 6ft 1in (1.85m)
WEIGHT: 234lbs (106kg)
HOMETOWN: Brooksville, Florida
SIGNATURE MOVE: Running Bo-Dog
RIVALS: Curtis Axel, Neville

BOBBY "THE BRAIN" HEENAN

Arguably the greatest manager in sports-entertainment history, Heenan guided countless Superstars to championship gold and was never afraid to interfere on their behalf.

HOMETOWN: Beverley Hills, California
SIGNATURE PHRASE: "You listen to me, you go to the top!"
RIVALS: Gorilla Monsoon, Big Boss Man

BOBBY FISH

As a member of the Undisputed ERA stable, Bobby Fish has made a major impact in NXT. He has defeated some of its greatest tag teams, winning the NXT Tag Team Title many times.

HEIGHT: 5ft 11in (1.80m)
WEIGHT: 197lbs (89kg)
HOMETOWN: Saratoga Springs, New York
SIGNATURE MOVE: Total Elimination
RIVALS: Imperium, Street Profits

BOBBY LASHLEY

"The All Mighty" Bobby Lashley is one of the most dynamic forces ever to compete in the WWE ring. An Intercontinental Champion, he has set his sights on the WWE Championship.

HEIGHT: 6ft 3in (1.91m)
WEIGHT: 273lbs (124kg)
HOMETOWN: Colorado Springs, Colorado
SIGNATURE MOVE: The Dominator
RIVALS: Drew McIntyre, Finn Bálor

One the most decorated WWE Superstars of all time, Booker T won multiple World Titles, tag team championships, and the *King of the Ring* tournament. He was inducted into the WWE Hall of Fame in 2013.

HEIGHT: 6ft 3in (1.91m)
WEIGHT: 256lbs (116kg)
HOMETOWN:
Houston, Texas
SIGNATURE MOVE:
Spinaroonie
RIVALS: Triple H,
Stone Cold Steve Austin

THE BOOGEYMAN

Whether he was foaming at the mouth or eating worms, The Boogeyman's unpredictable in-ring style grossed out his opponents so much that they couldn't defeat him.

HEIGHT: 6ft 2in (1.88m)
WEIGHT: 260lbs (118kg)
HOMETOWN: The Bottomless Pit
SIGNATURE MOVE: Boogeyslam
RIVALS: Booker T, Finlay

BRAUN STROWMAN

"The Monster Among Men" Braun Strowman stalks his prey in the ring. He began his WWE career as part of The Wyatt Family before dominating WWE alone.

HEIGHT: 6ft 8in (2.03m)
WEIGHT: 385lbs (175kg)
SIGNATURE MOVE:
Reverse Chokeslam
RIVALS: Roman Reigns, Brock Lesnar

BRAY WYATT

Once the leader of the Wyatt Family stable, Bray Wyatt has changed into the demonic "Fiend." He seeks to punish opponents and rivals who have wronged him over the years.

HEIGHT: 6ft 3in (1.91m)
WEIGHT: 285lbs (129kg)
SIGNATURE MOVE: Sister Abigail
RIVALS: John Cena, Randy Orton

BREEZANGO

A ballroom dancer and a supermodel make a very stylish tag team. While Breezango take in-ring competition seriously, they are more focused on exposing crimes of fashion in WWE.

COMBINED WEIGHT: 456lbs (207kg)
SIGNATURE MOVE: Beauty in Motion
RIVALS: The Usos

FANDANGO

TYLER BREEZE

BRET "HIT MAN" HART

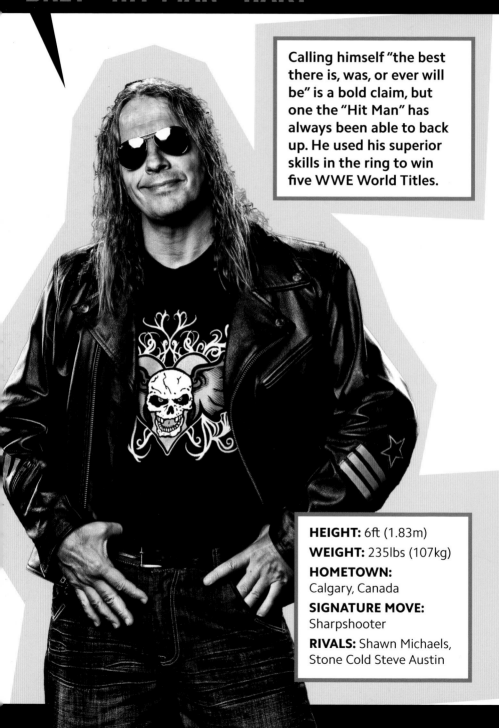

Calling himself "the best there is, was, or ever will be" is a bold claim, but one the "Hit Man" has always been able to back up. He used his superior skills in the ring to win five WWE World Titles.

HEIGHT: 6ft (1.83m)
WEIGHT: 235lbs (107kg)
HOMETOWN: Calgary, Canada
SIGNATURE MOVE: Sharpshooter
RIVALS: Shawn Michaels, Stone Cold Steve Austin

THE BRIAN KENDRICK

On his WWE debut in 2003, The Brian Kendrick amazed the WWE Universe with his high-flying moves. He left WWE in 2009, but returned with a vengeance seven years later.

HEIGHT: 5ft 8in (1.73m)
WEIGHT: 157lbs (71kg)
HOMETOWN: Venice, California
SIGNATURE MOVE: Captain's Hook
RIVALS: TJP, Akira Tozawa

BRITISH BULLDOG

British Bulldog Davey Boy Smith loved to showcase his strength in matches by lifting opponents above his head. He won several championships and became the first WWE European Champion.

HEIGHT: 5ft 11in (1.80m)
WEIGHT: 260lbs (118kg)
HOMETOWN: Manchester, England
SIGNATURE MOVE: Running Powerslam
RIVALS: Ken Shamrock, The Rock

They call him "The Beast," and Brock Lesnar lives up to his name. He has destroyed the very best Superstars in all of WWE, including the Undertaker and John Cena, and also dominated the mixed martial arts world.

HEIGHT: 6ft 3in (1.91m)
WEIGHT: 286lbs (130kg)
HOMETOWN: Minneapolis, Minnesota
SIGNATURE MOVE: German Suplex
RIVALS: Roman Reigns, Seth Rollins

BRONSON REED

"Aus-zilla" Bronson Reed has shown his tremendous strength and power in NXT UK. With his unique Australian Strong Style, he has conquered countless opponents in the ring.

HEIGHT: 5ft 11in (1.80m)
WEIGHT: 330lbs (150kg)
HOMETOWN: Black Forest, South Australia
SIGNATURE MOVE: Samoan Drop
RIVALS: Undisputed ERA, Cameron Grimes

THE BROTHERS OF DESTRUCTION

When these legendary Superstar brothers joined forces, their tag team combination sent devastating shockwaves throughout WWE.

COMBINED WEIGHT: 632lbs (287kg)
SIGNATURE MOVE: Double Chokeslam
RIVALS: D-Generation X, The Wyatt Family

KANE

UNDERTAKER

During his two reigns as WWE Champion, Bruno Sammartino defeated countless opponents, including "Superstar" Billy Graham and Gorilla Monsoon. The definition of an icon, Sammartino was inducted into the WWE Hall of Fame in 2013.

HEIGHT: 5ft 10in (1.78m)
WEIGHT: 265lbs (120kg)
HOMETOWN: Pittsburgh, Pennsylvania
SIGNATURE MOVE: Bear Hug
RIVALS: "Rowdy" Roddy Piper, "Macho Man" Randy Savage

BRUTUS BEEFCAKE

A talented Superstar known for his flamboyant outfits, Brutus "The Barber" Beefcake used barber clippers to shave the head of each of his vanquished opponents.

HEIGHT: 6ft 3in (1.91m)
WEIGHT: 272lbs (123kg)
HOMETOWN: San Francisco, California
SIGNATURE MOVE: Sleeper Hold
RIVALS: Mr. Perfect, IRS, "The Million Dollar Man" Ted DiBiase

THE BUSHWHACKERS

They may have had poor manners and toothless grins, but these Kiwi cousins were beloved by the WWE Universe. The Bushwhackers entered the WWE Hall of Fame in 2015.

COMBINED WEIGHT: 496lbs (225kg)
HOMETOWN: New Zealand
SIGNATURE MOVE: Battering Ram
RIVALS: The Natural Disasters, The Nasty Boys

BUTCH

LUKE

33

"The Monster Among Men" Braun Strowman demonstrates his Running Powerslam finisher on "The Glorious One" Robert Roode at *Monday Night RAW* (June 4, 2018).

BYRON SAXTON

Originally a competitor in NXT, Byron Saxton left in-ring competition behind and picked up a microphone. He is now one of the most trusted commentators in WWE.

HEIGHT: 6ft 1in (1.85m)
WEIGHT: 212lbs (96kg)
HOMETOWN: Burke, Virginia
RIVALS: Corey Graves

CAMERON GRIMES

With a bad attitude and legs like cinder blocks, Cameron Grimes fought his way into NXT. A second-generation competitor, he was inspired by his heroes The Hardy Boyz.

HEIGHT: 6ft (1.83m)
WEIGHT: 220lbs (100kg)
HOMETOWN: Burlington, North Carolina
SIGNATURE MOVE: Moonsault Slam
RIVALS: Finn Bálor

CANDICE LERAE

The NXT Universe first knew Candice LeRae as a sweet, cupcake-loving Superstar, but she grew tired of that image and adopted a more aggressive attitude as the "Poison Pixie."

HEIGHT: 5ft 2in (1.57m)
HOMETOWN: Anaheim, California
SIGNATURE MOVE: Quebrada
RIVALS: Mia Yim, Tegan Nox

CARMELLA

Carmella has introduced the WWE Universe to New York toughness. The first-ever Women's *Money in the Bank* winner cashed in to claim the *SmackDown* Women's Title.

HEIGHT: 5ft 5in (1.65m)
HOMETOWN:
Staten Island, New York
SIGNATURE MOVE: Code of Silence
RIVALS: Becky Lynch, Nikki Bella

CEDRIC ALEXANDER

Part of the WWE Cruiserweight Division, Cedric Alexander is known for his unique in-ring offensive style, which combines hard-hitting kicks and high-flying aerial maneuvers.

HEIGHT: 5ft 10in (1.78m)
WEIGHT: 205lbs (93kg)
HOMETOWN:
Charlotte, North Carolina
SIGNATURE MOVE: Lumbar Check
RIVALS: Noam Dar, TJP

CESARO

Fluent in five languages, Swiss native Cesaro is comfortable meeting fans all over the world. But there's nowhere that feels more like home to "The King of Swing" than the WWE ring.

HEIGHT: 6ft 5in (1.96m)
WEIGHT: 218lbs (99kg)
HOMETOWN:
Lucerne, Switzerland
SIGNATURE MOVE: Cesaro Swing
RIVALS: Sheamus, The Hardy Boyz

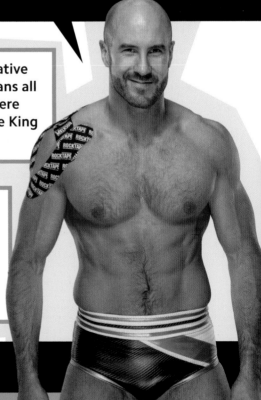

CHARLOTTE FLAIR

As the daughter of 16-time World Champion Ric Flair, Charlotte Flair is building her own legacy worthy of the family name. Having won an unprecedented 12 women's titles in WWE and NXT, she is truly the queen of WWE.

HEIGHT:
5ft 10in (1.78m)
HOMETOWN:
The Queen City
SIGNATURE MOVE:
Figure-Eight Leglock
RIVALS: Becky Lynch, Sasha Banks

CHARLY CARUSO

As a backstage interviewer at WWE events and the host of shows like *RAW Talk* and *This Week in WWE*, Charly Caruso always asks the right questions to get the scoop.

HEIGHT: 5ft 2in (1.57m)
HOMETOWN:
Indianapolis, Indiana
RIVALS: The IIconics

CHELSEA GREEN

After competing worldwide, Chelsea Green wanted to make a major impact at NXT. Though the NXT Women's Championship has proven elusive, Chelsea knows it's only a matter of time.

HEIGHT: 5ft 7in (1.70m)
HOMETOWN:
Victoria, Canada
SIGNATURE MOVE: Facebuster
RIVALS: Xia Li

CHIEF JAY STRONGBOW

A premier Superstar in the 1970s and 1980s, Chief Jay Strongbow retired from the ring in 1985, but returned to mentor fellow Native American WWE Superstar Tatanka.

HEIGHT: 6ft (1.83m)
WEIGHT: 247lbs (112kg)
HOMETOWN: Pawhuska, Oklahoma
SIGNATURE MOVE: Tomahawk Chop
RIVALS: The Wild Samoans

CHRISTIAN

Christian debuted alongside his best friend Edge in the 1990s. He won countless titles as a competitor before bringing *The Edge and Christian Show* to WWE Network.

HEIGHT: 6ft 2in (1.88m)
WEIGHT: 212lbs (96kg)
HOMETOWN: Toronto, Canada
SIGNATURE MOVE: The Killswitch
RIVALS: Randy Orton, Tommy Dreamer

Chyna had an illustrious career in WWE. She was the first female Intercontinental Champion, the first woman to enter the Men's Royal Rumble Match, and a founding member of the D-Generation X stable.

HEIGHT: 6ft (1.83m)
HOMETOWN: Londonderry, New Hampshire
SIGNATURE MOVE: Powerbomb
RIVALS: Jeff Jarrett, Ivory

COREY GRAVES

With experience as an in-ring competitor, Corey Graves brings a tremendous level of insight to his role as commentator on WWE's top programs and to his podcast, "After the Bell."

HEIGHT: 6ft 1in (1.85m)
WEIGHT: 209lbs (95kg)
HOMETOWN:
Pittsburgh, Pennsylvania
RIVALS: Byron Saxton, Michael Cole

"COWBOY" BOB ORTON

The second of three generations in WWE, "Cowboy" Bob Orton was a worthy successor to his father Bob Orton, Sr., and he passed the family legacy down to his son, Randy Orton.

HEIGHT: 6ft 1in (1.85m)
WEIGHT: 242lbs (110kg)
HOMETOWN: Kansas City, Kansas
SIGNATURE MOVE: Superplex
RIVALS: Don Muraco, Tito Santana

DAKOTA KAI

A proud Kiwi, Dakota Kai was once a member of Team Kick with Tegan Nox. After a serious knee injury, Dakota cut ties with her friend and adopted an aggressive new attitude.

HEIGHT: 5ft 6in (1.68m)
HOMETOWN: Auckland, New Zealand
SIGNATURE MOVE: Double Foot Stomp
RIVALS: Tegan Nox, Rhea Ripley

DAMIAN PRIEST

Aiming to bring destruction and chaos to NXT, "The Archer of Infamy" Damian Priest has targeted the best the brand has to offer, including Finn Bálor and Keith Lee.

HEIGHT:
6ft 5in (1.96m)
WEIGHT: 249lbs (113kg)
HOMETOWN: New York, New York
SIGNATURE MOVE: The Reckoning
RIVALS: Finn Bálor, Keith Lee

DANA BROOKE

With a background in bodybuilding, Dana Brooke has a physique that is unmatched in the WWE Women's Division. She is flexing her muscles in pursuit of championships.

HEIGHT: 5ft 3in (1.60m)
HOMETOWN: Cleveland, Ohio
SIGNATURE MOVE:
Handstand Leg Hold
RIVALS: Bayley, Charlotte Flair

DANNY BURCH

This powerhouse grappler is a force to be reckoned with in NXT and NXT UK. Since aligning himself with Oney Lorcan, Danny Burch has set his sights on the NXT Tag Team Titles.

HEIGHT: 6ft (1.83m)
WEIGHT: 190lbs (86kg)
HOMETOWN: London, England
SIGNATURE MOVE: The London Bridge
RIVALS: Drew Gulak, Imperium

DANIEL BRYAN

Ever the underdog, Daniel Bryan won the love and respect of the WWE Universe with his rallying "Yes!" chant. He became an inspirational hero, winning countless titles.

HEIGHT: 5ft 10in (1.78m)
WEIGHT: 210lbs (95kg)
HOMETOWN: Aberdeen, Washington
SIGNATURE MOVE: Yes Lock
RIVALS: Triple H, The Miz

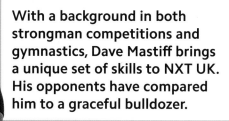

DAVE MASTIFF

With a background in both strongman competitions and gymnastics, Dave Mastiff brings a unique set of skills to NXT UK. His opponents have compared him to a graceful bulldozer.

HEIGHT: 5ft 10in (1.78m)
WEIGHT: 322lbs (146kg)
HOMETOWN: The Black Country, England
SIGNATURE MOVE: Discus Lariat
RIVALS: Joe Coffey, Imperium

DAVID OTUNGA

He is a talented in-ring competitor, but David Otunga's biggest strengths lie outside the ring. A trained lawyer, he has helped WWE's General Managers fight legal battles.

HEIGHT: 6ft (1.83m)
WEIGHT: 229lbs (104kg)
HOMETOWN: Hollywood, California
SIGNATURE MOVE: The Verdict
RIVALS: John Cena, Jerry "The King" Lawler

DEXTER LUMIS

Sadistic yet extremely talented, Dexter Lumis is a rising star in NXT. He enjoys inflicting the most ruthless pain on his opponents and rivals—both in and out of the ring.

HEIGHT: 6ft 2in (1.88m)
WEIGHT: 239lbs (108kg)
HOMETOWN: Jacksonville, Florida
SIGNATURE MOVE:
Diving Leg Drop
RIVALS: Undisputed ERA

D-GENERATION X

Rebellious and fun-loving, D-Generation X ushered in the Attitude Era. Original members Shawn Michaels and Triple H soon brought other Superstars into the stable, including X-Pac, Chyna, and New Age Outlaws.

COMBINED WEIGHT:
480lbs (218kg)
SIGNATURE MOVES: Sweet Chin Music, The Pedigree
RIVALS: The Brothers of Destruction, Mr. McMahon

X-PAC

CHYNA

DIAMOND DALLAS PAGE

A three-time WCW World Champion, Diamond Dallas Page was nearly 40 years old when he began his in-ring career, but nothing could stop him fulfilling his WWE dreams.

HEIGHT: 6ft 5in (1.96m)
WEIGHT: 248lbs (112kg)
HOMETOWN: The Jersey Shore, New Jersey
SIGNATURE MOVE: Diamond Cutter
RIVALS: "Macho Man" Randy Savage, Undertaker

SHAWN MICHAELS

ROAD DOGG

TRIPLE H

BILLY GUNN

DIESEL

He rose to the top of WWE by becoming WWE Champion, but Diesel's biggest impact came when he "took over" WCW as one of the founding members of the nWo faction.

HEIGHT: 6ft 10in (2.08m)
WEIGHT: 328lbs (149kg)
HOMETOWN: Detroit, Michigan
SIGNATURE MOVE:
Jackknife Powerbomb
RIVALS: Big Show, Undertaker

D'LO BROWN

By bobbing his head from side to side, D'Lo Brown fired up the WWE Universe. A pectoral injury led D'Lo to wear a chest protector, which he used to increase the impact of his Lo Down move.

HEIGHT: 6ft 1in (1.85m)
WEIGHT: 268lbs (122kg)
HOMETOWN: Chicago, Illinois
SIGNATURE MOVE: Lo Down
RIVALS: Raven, D-Generation X

DOLPH ZIGGLER

Nicknamed "The Show Off," Dolph Ziggler's brash attitude and impressive talent have helped him garner several championships in WWE— and his fair share of enemies.

HEIGHT: 6ft (1.83m)
WEIGHT: 218lbs (99kg)
HOMETOWN: Hollywood, Florida
SIGNATURE MOVE: The Zig Zag
RIVALS: Drew McIntyre, Roman Reigns

DOMINIK DIJAKOVIC

A star athlete in high school and college, Dominik Dijakovic competed on the independent wrestling scene before joining NXT, where he's proven to be a powerhouse to watch.

HEIGHT: 6ft 7in (2.01m)
WEIGHT: 270lbs (122kg)
HOMETOWN: Worcester, Massachusetts
SIGNATURE MOVE: Chokeslam Backbreaker
RIVALS: Velveteen Dream, Undisputed ERA

DON MURACO

With a total disregard for the WWE rulebook, Don Muraco was despised by many. But that disdain only seemed to motivate the two-time Intercontinental Champion.

HEIGHT: 6ft 3in (1.91m)
WEIGHT: 275lbs (125kg)
HOMETOWN: Sunset Beach, Hawaii
SIGNATURE MOVE: Asiatic Spike
RIVALS: Ricky "The Dragon" Steamboat, Bob Backlund

DREW GULAK

Known for his toughness, Drew Gulak never wears knee or elbow pads in the ring. His conservative technical style focuses on submission holds and mat grappling.

HEIGHT: 6ft (1.83m)
WEIGHT: 193lbs (88kg)
HOMETOWN: Philadelphia, Pennsylvania
SIGNATURE MOVE: Dragon Sleeper
RIVALS: Rich Swann, Cedric Alexander

DUSTY RHODES

The true "American Dream," Dusty Rhodes was a regular hardworking guy who found great success in sports entertainment. The WWE Universe saw themselves in him and celebrated his victories as their own.

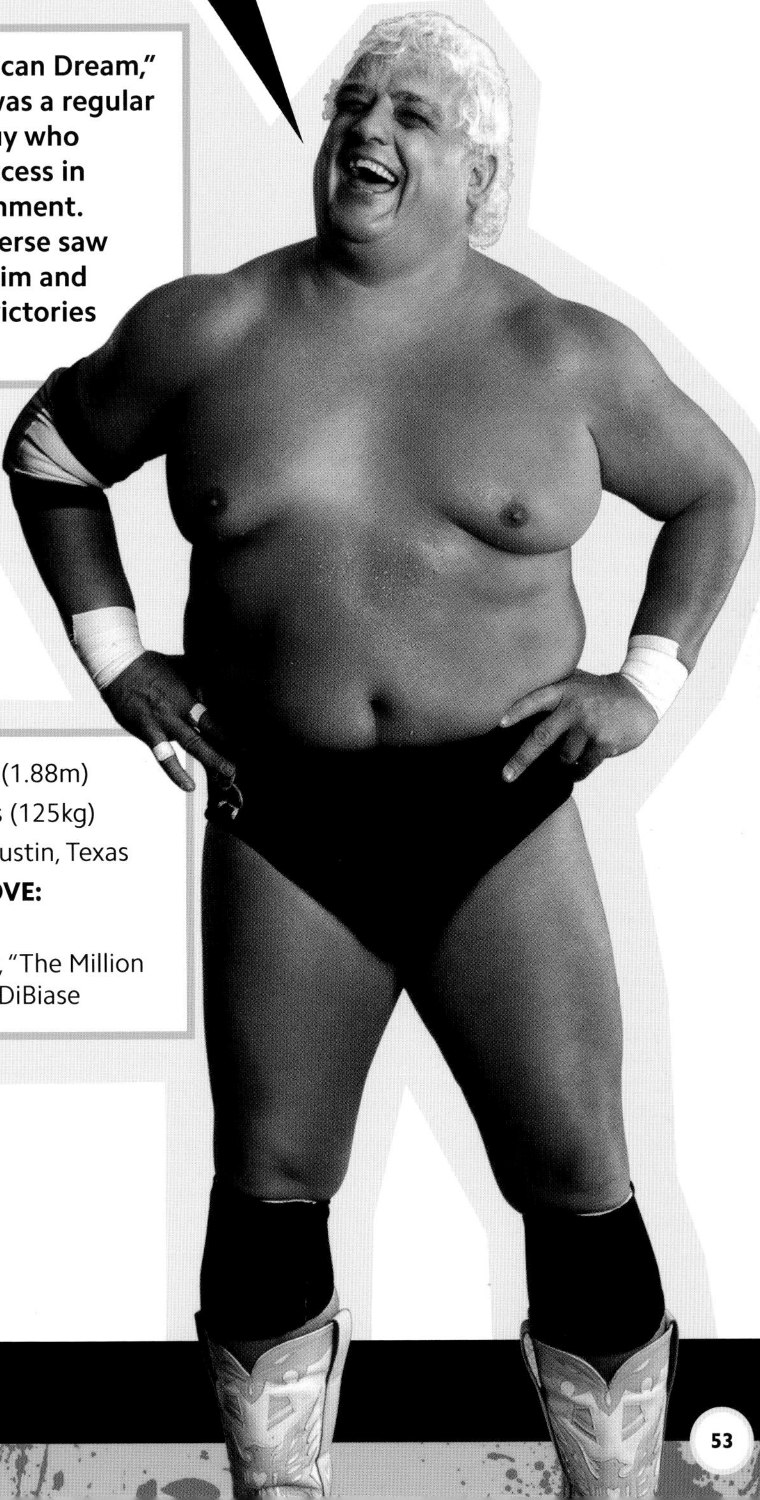

HEIGHT: 6ft 2in (1.88m)

WEIGHT: 275lbs (125kg)

HOMETOWN: Austin, Texas

SIGNATURE MOVE:
Bionic Elbow

RIVALS: Ric Flair, "The Million Dollar Man" Ted DiBiase

DREW MCINTYRE

Once called "The Chosen One," Drew McIntyre left WWE to refine his in-ring skills. On his return in 2017, he captured the NXT Title before becoming WWE Champion in 2020.

HEIGHT: 6ft 5in (1.96m)
WEIGHT: 254lbs (115kg)
HOMETOWN: Ayr, Scotland
SIGNATURE MOVE: Claymore Kick
RIVALS: Seth Rollins, Brock Lesnar

EARTHQUAKE

Earthquake rocked the ring each time he set foot in it. With his devastating Earthquake Splash, he put countless Superstars out of action.

HEIGHT: 6ft 7in (2.01m)
WEIGHT: 468lbs (212kg)
HOMETOWN: Vancouver, Canada
SIGNATURE MOVE: Earthquake Splash
RIVALS: Hulk Hogan, Legion of Doom

With a knack for exploiting shortcuts to great success, Edge always makes the right decision at the right time. An injury forced him to retire in 2011, but Edge made a shocking return to action in 2020.

HEIGHT: 6ft 5in (1.96m)
WEIGHT: 241lbs (109kg)
HOMETOWN: Toronto, Canada
SIGNATURE MOVE: Spear
RIVALS: Randy Orton, Undertaker

EDGE AND CHRISTIAN

Childhood friends Edge and Christian had a shared dream of competing in WWE together. They burst onto the scene in the late 1990s and have battled (and made their comedy sketch show) side by side ever since.

COMBINED WEIGHT: 453lbs (205kg)

HOMETOWN: Toronto, Canada

SIGNATURE MOVE: Five-Second Pose

RIVALS: The Dudley Boyz, The Hardy Boyz

CHRISTIAN

EDGE

EDDIE GUERRERO

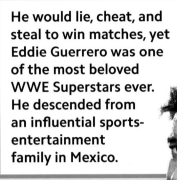

He would lie, cheat, and steal to win matches, yet Eddie Guerrero was one of the most beloved WWE Superstars ever. He descended from an influential sports-entertainment family in Mexico.

HEIGHT: 5ft 8in (1.73m)
WEIGHT: 220lbs (100kg)
HOMETOWN:
El Paso, Texas
SIGNATURE MOVE:
Frog Splash
RIVALS: Brock Lesnar, Kurt Angle

EDDIE DENNIS

Former school headmaster Eddie Dennis left education to pursue his dream of sports entertainment. His brilliant mind is constantly strategizing ways to win matches in NXT UK.

HEIGHT: 6ft 6in (1.98m)
WEIGHT: 230lbs (104kg)
HOMETOWN: Swansea, Wales
SIGNATURE MOVE: Inverted DDT
RIVALS: Dave Mastiff

ELIAS

Elias can often be found with his guitar in the ring, singing about whatever town he's in and insulting his opponents. But when it's time to compete, Elias really lets loose.

HEIGHT: 6ft (1.83m)
WEIGHT: 217lbs (98kg)
HOMETOWN: Pittsburgh, Pennsylvania
SIGNATURE MOVE: Swinging Neckbreaker
RIVALS: Kassius Ohno, Apollo Crews

ELIZABETH

Manager and occasional competitor Miss Elizabeth guided "Macho Man" Randy Savage to the WWE Championship, then married him at *SummerSlam 1991* in "The Match Made in Heaven."

HEIGHT: 5ft 4in (1.63m)
HOMETOWN: Louisville, Kentucky
RIVALS: Sensational Sherri, Kimberly Page

EMBER MOON

Striking with catlike precision, Ember Moon hits hard and fast. A former NXT Women's Champion, she now has her sights set on the *RAW* and *SmackDown* Women's Titles.

HEIGHT: 5ft 2in (1.57m)
HOMETOWN: Dallas, Texas
SIGNATURE MOVE: The Eclipse
RIVALS: Bayley, Sonya Deville

EVE

A trained martial artist with a degree in engineering, Eve is dangerous on multiple levels. After joining WWE in 2007, she went on to win the Divas Championship three times.

HEIGHT: 5ft 8in (1.73m)
HOMETOWN: Denver, Colorado
SIGNATURE MOVE: Evesault
RIVALS: Natalya, Brie Bella

EVER-RISE

Despite their name and success on the independent scene, Ever-Rise still have a steep mountain to climb in NXT, but they plan to keep on rising.

COMBINED WEIGHT: 403lbs (183kg)
SIGNATURE MOVE: Double DDT
RIVALS: Breezango, Oney Lorcan, Danny Burch

MATT MARTEL

CHASE PARKER

EVOLUTION

This fierce stable took over WWE in the early 2000s and showcased the best of the past, present, and future of sports entertainment. All champions, together they were legendary.

COMBINED WEIGHT: 1038lbs (471kg)
SIGNATURE MOVE: Evolution Beatdown
RIVALS: The Shield, Goldberg

RIC FLAIR

TRIPLE H

BATISTA

RANDY ORTON

FABIAN AICHNER

This Italian Superstar describes himself in one word: intense. Fabian Aichner joined NXT UK to dominate it. His alliance with the Imperium stable led him to win the NXT Tag Team Titles.

HEIGHT: 6ft (1.83m)
WEIGHT: 220lbs (100kg)
HOMETOWN: South Tyrol, Italy
SIGNATURE MOVE: Frog Splash
RIVALS: British Strong Style, Undisputed ERA

FAAROOQ

In a career that spanned 20 years, Faarooq made sports-entertainment history as the first African American World Heavyweight Champion when he won the WCW title.

HEIGHT: 6ft 2in (1.88m)
WEIGHT: 270lbs (122kg)
HOMETOWN:
Warner Robins, Georgia
SIGNATURE MOVE: Dominator
RIVALS: Lex Luger, The Rock

FINLAY

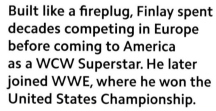

Built like a fireplug, Finlay spent decades competing in Europe before coming to America as a WCW Superstar. He later joined WWE, where he won the United States Championship.

HEIGHT: 6ft 2in (1.88m)
WEIGHT: 233lbs (106kg)
HOMETOWN:
Belfast, Northern Ireland
SIGNATURE MOVE: Celtic Cross
RIVALS: Booker T, William Regal

FINN BÁLOR

After making his name in Ireland and Japan, Finn Bálor made an immediate impact when he joined NXT, winning the NXT Championship and the first-ever Dusty Rhodes Tag Team Classic.

HEIGHT: 5ft 11in (1.80m)
WEIGHT: 190lbs (86kg)
HOMETOWN: Bray, Ireland
SIGNATURE MOVE: Coup de Grâce
RIVALS: Bray Wyatt, Kevin Owens

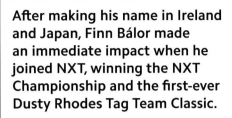

"FLASH" MORGAN WEBSTER

With a love for 1960s British style, "Flash" Morgan Webster calls himself the "MODfather." He uses an aerial fighting style but can also grapple with the best of them.

HEIGHT: 5ft 9in (1.75m)
WEIGHT: 156lbs (71kg)
HOMETOWN: Brynmawr, Wales
SIGNATURE MOVE: Britpop Drop
RIVALS: Zack Gibson, James Drake

THE FORGOTTEN SONS

JAXSON RYKER

STEVE CUTLER

WESLEY BLAKE

After battling the tag teams on NXT, The Forgotten Sons joined *SmackDown*, promising to take the Tag Team Titles away from the likes of The New Day and The Usos.

COMBINED WEIGHT: 710lbs (322kg)
SIGNATURE MOVE: Lost and Damned
RIVALS: Street Profits, Heavy Machinery

FREDDIE BLASSIE

"Classy" Freddie Blassie took the best Superstars in WWE history all the way to the top. He carried a cane with him to the ring and he wasn't afraid to use it as a weapon.

HEIGHT: 5ft 10in (1.78m)
WEIGHT: 220lbs (100kg)
HOMETOWN: Hollywood, California
RIVALS: Hulk Hogan, Gorilla Monsoon

GALLUS

After becoming a destructive force on the European independent wrestling scene, the Gallus faction set out to take over NXT UK and win the Tag Team Titles.

JOE COFFEY

MARK COFFEY

WOLFGANG

COMBINED WEIGHT: 741lbs (336kg)
SIGNATURE MOVE: Combined Lariats
RIVALS: Imperium, Dave Mastiff

GENE OKERLUND

Arguably the best interviewer in sports-entertainment history, "Mean" Gene Okerlund always got to the bottom of rumors and news with his probing questions.

HEIGHT: 5ft 9in (1.75m)
WEIGHT: 213lbs (97kg)
HOMETOWN: Sarasota, Florida
RIVALS: "Rowdy" Roddy Piper, Mr. Fuji

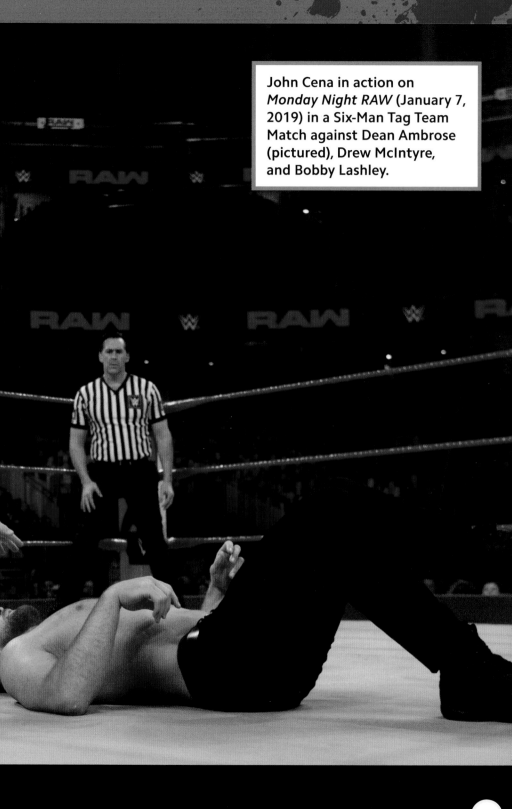

John Cena in action on *Monday Night RAW* (January 7, 2019) in a Six-Man Tag Team Match against Dean Ambrose (pictured), Drew McIntyre, and Bobby Lashley.

GEORGE "THE ANIMAL" STEELE

Despite his nickname, George "The Animal" Steele was surprisingly gentle. But, like any animal, don't make him angry! He was known for his trademark green tongue.

HEIGHT: 6ft 1in (1.85m)
WEIGHT: 275lbs (125kg)
HOMETOWN: Detroit, Michigan
SIGNATURE MOVE: Flying Hammerlock
RIVALS: "Macho Man" Randy Savage, Bruno Sammartino

GERALD BRISCO

An NWA World Heavyweight Champion, Gerald "Jerry" Brisco joined WWE in the 1980s and formed a dynamic tag team with his brother, Jack. He later became an important executive in WWE.

HEIGHT: 6ft (1.83m)
WEIGHT: 209lbs (95kg)
HOMETOWN: Blackwell, Oklahoma
SIGNATURE MOVE: Figure-Four Leglock
RIVALS: Ricky "The Dragon" Steamboat

THE GODFATHER

Followed to the ring by his "Train" of beautiful women, The Godfather was a happy-go-lucky Superstar who loved life and WWE. The WWE Universe, in turn, loved him.

HEIGHT: 6ft 6in (1.98m)
WEIGHT: 330lbs (150kg)
HOMETOWN: Las Vegas, Nevada
SIGNATURE MOVE: Pimp Drop
RIVALS: Undertaker

THE GOON

Hockey might be a violent sport, but The Goon was too aggressive even for that. He made his way to WWE, where he found an outlet for his violent tendencies.

HEIGHT: 6ft 1in (1.85m)
WEIGHT: 250lbs (113kg)
HOMETOWN: Duluth, Minnesota
SIGNATURE MOVE: Cross Check
RIVALS: Undertaker, The Stalker

GOLDBERG

"Who's next?" was the battle cry that defined Goldberg's career. A former WCW, WWE World Heavyweight, and WWE Universal Champion, Goldberg has plowed through the biggest names in sports entertainment.

HEIGHT: 6ft 4in (1.93m)
WEIGHT: 285lbs (129kg)
HOMETOWN: Atlanta, Georgia
SIGNATURE MOVE: Jackhammer
RIVALS: Brock Lesnar, Kevin Owens

GORILLA MONSOON

Following a legendary in-ring career that saw him challenge Bruno Sammartino and André the Giant, Gorilla Monsoon became an iconic voice of WWE as a commentator.

HEIGHT: 6ft 7in (2.01m)
WEIGHT: 401lbs (182kg)
HOMETOWN: Manchuria
SIGNATURE MOVE: Airplane Spin
RIVALS: Bruno Sammartino, André the Giant

GREG HAMILTON

WWE ring announcer Greg Hamilton has the power to make Superstars look great, whether he's introducing them on their way to the ring or crowning a new champion.

HEIGHT: 5ft 10in (1.78m)
HOMETOWN: Butler County, Ohio
RIVALS: Shane McMahon

GREG "THE HAMMER" VALENTINE

A legend in the ring, Greg "The Hammer" Valentine's rivalries with the likes of "Rowdy" Roddy Piper and Don Muraco were epic. He won the Intercontinental and Tag Team Championships.

HEIGHT: 6ft (1.83m)
WEIGHT: 243lbs (110kg)
HOMETOWN: Seattle, Washington
SIGNATURE MOVE: Figure-Four Leglock
RIVALS: "Rowdy" Roddy Piper, Don Muraco

GRIZZLED YOUNG VETERANS

This talented duo won the inaugural NXT UK Tag Team Championship and became the title's longest-reigning champions.

WEIGHT: 401lbs (182kg)
SIGNATURE MOVE: Ticket to Mayhem
RIVALS: Gallus, Moustache Mountain

JAMES DRAKE

ZACK GIBSON

"HACKSAW" JIM DUGGAN

One of the most patriotic Superstars in WWE, "Hacksaw" Jim Duggan led the WWE Universe in chants of "USA!" during every match he ever had.

HEIGHT: 6ft 3in (1.91m)
WEIGHT: 270lbs (122kg)
HOMETOWN: Glens Falls, New York
SIGNATURE MOVE: Three-Point Stance Clothesline
RIVALS: Diamond Dallas Page, Sgt. Slaughter

HARLEM HEAT

Brothers Booker T and Stevie Ray ruled WCW's tag team division in the 1990s, winning the WCW Tag Team Championship an unprecedented ten times.

COMBINED WEIGHT: 545lbs (247kg)
SIGNATURE MOVES: Ax Kick, Flapjack
RIVALS: The Nasty Boys, The Outsiders

STEVIE RAY

BOOKER T

HARLEY RACE

With seven World Heavyweight Titles, Harley Race made a solid case for his claim that he was once the greatest Superstar on Earth. He was known for being tough as nails in the ring.

HEIGHT: 6ft 1in (1.85m)
WEIGHT: 253lbs (115kg)
HOMETOWN: Kansas City, Missouri
SIGNATURE MOVE: Piledriver
RIVALS: Ric Flair, Junkyard Dog

THE HART FOUNDATION

Brothers-in-law Bret "Hit Man" Hart and Jim "The Anvil" Neidhart were one of the greatest tag teams ever. The Hart Foundation were trained by Bret's father, WWE Hall of Famer Stu Hart.

COMBINED WEIGHT: 516lbs (234kg)
SIGNATURE MOVE: Hart Attack
RIVALS: British Bulldogs, The Nasty Boys

BRET "HIT MAN" HART

JIM "THE ANVIL" NEIDHART

HEAVY MACHINERY

Like wrecking balls, Heavy Machinery cause maximum damage in WWE. They roll forward and knock down their competition on *SmackDown*, to cheers from the WWE Universe.

TUCKER

OTIS

COMBINED WEIGHT: 592lbs (269kg)
SIGNATURE MOVE: Boom Shaka Loo
RIVALS: AOP, The Miz and John Morrison

"HIGH CHIEF" PETER MAIVIA

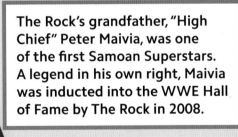

The Rock's grandfather, "High Chief" Peter Maivia, was one of the first Samoan Superstars. A legend in his own right, Maivia was inducted into the WWE Hall of Fame by The Rock in 2008.

HEIGHT: 5ft 9in (1.75m)
WEIGHT: 275lbs (125kg)
HOMETOWN: Samoa
SIGNATURE MOVE: Stump Puller
RIVALS: Bob Backlund, "Superstar" Billy Graham

THE HONKY TONK MAN

Often mistaken for the late "King of Rock 'n' Roll" Elvis Presley, The Honky Tonk Man would often perform a song and dance number in the ring before getting down to business.

HEIGHT: 6ft 1in (1.85m)
WEIGHT: 243lbs (110kg)
HOMETOWN: Memphis, Tennessee
SIGNATURE MOVE: Shake, Rattle, and Roll
RIVALS: Ricky "The Dragon" Steamboat, The Ultimate Warrior

HOWARD FINKEL

Nicknamed "The Fink," Howard Finkel is the best-known ring announcer in WWE history. His distinctive voice echoes in arenas and stadiums when he calls out "neeeeew" champions.

HEIGHT: 5ft 8in (1.73m)
HOMETOWN: Newark, New Jersey

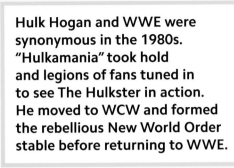

HULK HOGAN

Hulk Hogan and WWE were synonymous in the 1980s. "Hulkamania" took hold and legions of fans tuned in to see The Hulkster in action. He moved to WCW and formed the rebellious New World Order stable before returning to WWE.

HEIGHT: 6ft 7in (2.01m)
WEIGHT: 302lbs (137kg)
HOMETOWN: Venice Beach, California
SIGNATURE MOVE: Leg Drop
RIVALS: André the Giant, "Rowdy" Roddy Piper

HUMBERTO CARRILLO

A third-generation competitor, Humberto Carrillo learned his family's craft in Mexico. Since joining NXT and WWE, he's had a series of victories and is now aiming for championship gold.

HEIGHT: 6ft 1in (1.85m)
WEIGHT: 198lbs (90kg)
HOMETOWN: Monterrey, Mexico
SIGNATURE MOVE: Moonsault
RIVALS: Andrade, Angel Garza

THE HURRICANE

He was mild-mannered behind the scenes, but when Gregory Helms entered the arena, he became The Hurricane—a Superstar superhero who fought for truth and justice in the ring.

HEIGHT: 6ft (1.83m)
WEIGHT: 200lbs (91kg)
HOMETOWN: Raleigh, North Carolina
SIGNATURE MOVE: Eye of the Hurricane
RIVALS: The Rock, Matt Hardy

THE IICONICS

Best friends The IIconics grew up together, trained for WWE together, signed NXT contracts together, and won the Women's Tag Team Championship—together!

HOMETOWN: Sydney, Australia

SIGNATURE MOVE: IIconic Double Team

RIVALS: The Kabuki Warriors, Nikki Cross, Alexa Bliss

BILLY KAYE

PEYTON ROYCE

ILJA DRAGUNOV

Intensity and aggression drive Ilja Dragunov. The Russian competitor's devastating Torpedo Moscow maneuver has put down some of the best Superstars in NXT UK.

HEIGHT: 5ft 10in (1.78m)

WEIGHT: 198lbs (90kg)

HOMETOWN: Moscow, Russia

SIGNATURE MOVE: Torpedo Moscow

RIVALS: Gallus, Joe Coffey

IMPERIUM

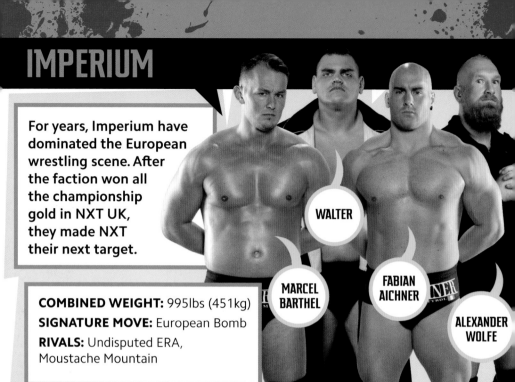

For years, Imperium have dominated the European wrestling scene. After the faction won all the championship gold in NXT UK, they made NXT their next target.

WALTER

MARCEL BARTHEL

FABIAN AICHNER

ALEXANDER WOLFE

COMBINED WEIGHT: 995lbs (451kg)
SIGNATURE MOVE: European Bomb
RIVALS: Undisputed ERA, Moustache Mountain

THE INDUS SHER

This mysterious and aggressive pair from India burst into NXT, attacking the reigning Tag Team Champions. With manager Malcolm Bivens by their side, no tag team is safe from The Indus Sher.

RINKU

SAURAV

MALCOLM BIVENS

COMBINED WEIGHT: 575lbs (261kg)
SIGNATURE MOVE: Elbow Drop Backbreaker
RIVALS: Matt Riddle, Ever-Rise

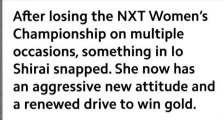

IO SHIRAI

After losing the NXT Women's Championship on multiple occasions, something in Io Shirai snapped. She now has an aggressive new attitude and a renewed drive to win gold.

HEIGHT: 5ft 1in (1.55m)
HOMETOWN: Tokyo, Japan
SIGNATURE MOVE: Moonsault
RIVALS: Candice LeRae, Shayna Baszler

THE IRON SHEIK

On a mission to prove his country's dominance over the rest of the world, the Iron Sheik used whatever underhanded tactics he could to claim victories for Iran.

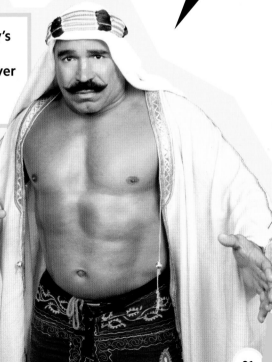

HEIGHT: 6ft (1.83m)
WEIGHT: 258lbs (117kg)
HOMETOWN: Tehran, Iran
SIGNATURE MOVE: Camel Clutch
RIVALS: Sgt. Slaughter, Bob Backlund

IRS

With no tolerance for anyone who cheats on their taxes (even if he cheats in his matches), IRS is a skilled and savvy technician. He calculates the best strategies to defeat his opponents.

HEIGHT: 6ft 3in (1.91m)
WEIGHT: 248lbs (112kg)
HOMETOWN: Washington, D.C.
SIGNATURE MOVE: The Write-Off
RIVALS: Big Boss Man, Tatanka

ISAIAH "SWERVE" SCOTT

When he joined NXT as part of the inaugural NXT Breakout tournament, Isaiah "Swerve" Scott had everything to prove. Lightning quick in the ring, he defeats opponents in minutes.

HEIGHT: 6ft 1in (1.85m)
WEIGHT: 201lbs (91kg)
HOMETOWN: Tacoma, Washington
SIGNATURE MOVE: Swerve Stomp
RIVALS: Drew Gulak, Angel Garza

ISLA DAWN

Describing herself as a "modern-day witch," Isla Dawn performs magically in the ring. Formerly a stage actor, she brings a unique element of drama to NXT UK.

HEIGHT: 5ft 7in (1.70m)
HOMETOWN: Glasgow, Scotland
SIGNATURE MOVE: Air Raid Crash
RIVALS: Toni Storm, Killer Kelly

JASON JORDAN

After winning championships in collegiate wrestling, Jason Jordan brought his tremendous talent and experience to NXT and WWE. He became a multi-time tag team champion.

HEIGHT: 6ft 3in (1.91m)
WEIGHT: 245lbs (111kg)
HOMETOWN: Chicago, Illinois
SIGNATURE MOVE: Grand Amplitude
RIVALS: The Miz, Seth Rollins

JAKE "THE SNAKE" ROBERTS

A master manipulator, Jake "The Snake" Roberts attacked his opponents both physically and psychologically. He was known to celebrate victories by letting his pet snakes slither all over his defeated adversaries.

HEIGHT: 6ft 6in (1.98m)
WEIGHT: 249lbs (113kg)
HOMETOWN:
Stone Mountain, Georgia
SIGNATURE MOVE: DDT
RIVALS: Ricky "The Dragon" Steamboat, "Macho Man" Randy Savage

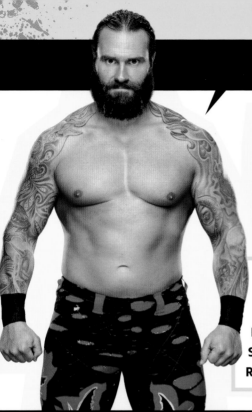

JAXSON RYKER

With a nasty attitude and a hard-hitting style, Jaxson Ryker of The Forgotten Sons stable takes no prisoners in the ring. He is a former member of the United States Marine Corps.

HEIGHT: 6ft 1in (1.85m)
WEIGHT: 245lbs (111kg)
HOMETOWN: Hickory, North Carolina
SIGNATURE MOVE: No Remorse
RIVALS: Street Profits, Heavy Machinery

JEFF HARDY

"The Charismatic Enigma" Jeff Hardy is a wonder to behold. With his colorful ring gear and face paint and his spectacular aerial style, Hardy has wowed fans and won countless titles.

HEIGHT: 6ft 1in (1.85m)
WEIGHT: 225lbs (102kg)
HOMETOWN: Cameron, North Carolina
SIGNATURE MOVE: Swanton Bomb
RIVALS: Randy Orton, Sheamus

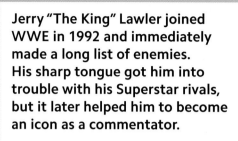

Jerry "The King" Lawler joined
WWE in 1992 and immediately
made a long list of enemies.
His sharp tongue got him into
trouble with his Superstar rivals,
but it later helped him to become
an icon as a commentator.

HEIGHT: 6ft (1.83m)
WEIGHT:
243lbs (110kg)
HOMETOWN:
Memphis, Tennessee
SIGNATURE MOVE:
Flying Fistdrop
RIVALS: Bret "Hit
Man" Hart, Jake
"The Snake" Roberts

JESSAMYN DUKE

One of the Four Horsewomen of MMA, Jessamyn Duke had an accomplished career in mixed martial arts before joining NXT. Whether alone or with her faction, Duke is always a powerful contender.

HEIGHT: 5ft 11in (1.80m)
HOMETOWN: Letcher County, Kentucky
SIGNATURE MOVE: Roundhouse Kick
RIVALS: Kairi Sane, Rhea Ripley

JIM "THE ANVIL" NEIDHART

Jim "The Anvil" Neidhart got his start in Calgary, Canada. Alongside his brother-in-law Bret "Hit Man" Hart, Neidhart won the WWE Tag Team Championship twice.

HEIGHT: 6ft 2in (1.88m)
WEIGHT: 281lbs (127kg)
HOMETOWN: Reno, Nevada
SIGNATURE MOVE: Anvil Flattener
RIVALS: The Nasty Boys, The Natural Disasters

JIMMY HART

Jimmy Hart has managed the very best in WWE, from Hulk Hogan to the Hart Foundation. He used his hateful megaphone to shout instructions to his charges during matches.

HEIGHT: 5ft 10in (1.78m)
WEIGHT: 166lbs (75kg)
HOMETOWN: Memphis, Tennessee
RIVALS: Hart Foundation, Big Boss Man

JINDER MAHAL

After years as an underdog and as part of less-than-successful tag teams, Jinder Mahal shocked the world in 2017 by defeating Randy Orton for the WWE World Heavyweight Championship.

HEIGHT: 6ft 5in (1.96m)
WEIGHT: 238lbs (108kg)
HOMETOWN: Punjab, India
SIGNATURE MOVE: Khallas
RIVALS: Randy Orton, Darren Young

JINNY

This fashionista has brought her knowledge of all things posh to NXT UK. A fierce competitor, Jinny plans to make the Women's Championship her ultimate accessory.

HEIGHT: 5ft 6in (1.68m)
HOMETOWN: London, England
SIGNATURE MOVE: The Facelift
RIVALS: Toni Storm, Xia Brookside

JOAQUIN WILDE

After overcoming a life-threatening injury, Joaquin Wilde proved his toughness both in and out of the ring. He has now joined forces with Santos Escobar.

HEIGHT: 5ft 7in (1.70m)
WEIGHT: 180lbs (82kg)
HOMETOWN: Chicago, Illinois
SIGNATURE MOVE: DDT
RIVALS: Kushida, Angel Garza

JOHN CENA

He is simultaneously loved and hated, but all that matters to John Cena is that he's the best. He's been the face of WWE for over a decade, winning titles and beating every Superstar that's sought to challenge him.

HEIGHT: 6ft 1in (1.85m)
WEIGHT: 251lbs (114kg)
HOMETOWN: West Newbury, Massachusetts
SIGNATURE MOVE: Attitude Adjustment
RIVALS: The Rock, AJ Styles

JOE COFFEY

Tough as nails and with an attitude to match, Joe Coffey is a powerful Scottish Superstar who garnered in-ring accolades throughout Europe and Japan before arriving in NXT UK.

HEIGHT: 5ft 11in (1.80m)
WEIGHT: 242lbs (110kg)
HOMETOWN: Glasgow, Scotland
SIGNATURE MOVE: Discus Lariat
RIVALS: Imperium, British Strong Style

JOHN MORRISON

The "Shaman of Sexy" returned to WWE in 2019 after years away and reminded the WWE Universe why he was popular in the first place: his parkour-style moves in the ring.

HEIGHT: 6ft (1.83m)
WEIGHT: 215lbs (98kg)
HOMETOWN: Los Angeles, California
SIGNATURE MOVE: Starship Pain
RIVALS: The New Day, The Usos

JOHNNY GARGANO

Formerly one half of the tag team #DIY, Johnny Gargano proved his individual greatness to the NXT Universe by winning the North American and NXT Championships.

HEIGHT: 5ft 10in (1.78m)
WEIGHT: 199lbs (90kg)
HOMETOWN: Cleveland, Ohio
SIGNATURE MOVE: Gargano Escape
RIVALS: Tommaso Ciampa, The Revival

JOHNNY SAINT

He began his career as a hard-hitting Superstar in the 1950s, competing all over Europe. Now, Johnny Saint brings his vast experience to his role as NXT UK General Manager.

HEIGHT: 5ft 8in (1.73m)
WEIGHT: 154lbs (70kg)
HOMETOWN: Manchester, England
RIVALS: Imperium

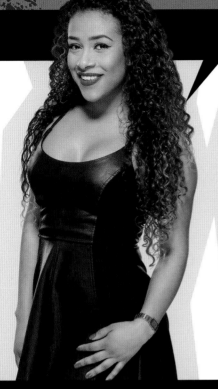

JOJO

After debuting as a dancer for Superstars' entrances, Jojo joined the *Total Divas* cast on the reality show's first season. She later became a fan-favorite ring announcer in NXT.

HEIGHT: 5ft 2in (1.57m)
HOMETOWN: Los Angeles, California
RIVALS: Tamina

JONATHAN COACHMAN

A brilliant sports analyst, "The Coach" was a longtime commentator on *RAW*. After a stint at ESPN, he returned to WWE to host pay-per-view kickoff shows on WWE Network.

HEIGHT: 6ft 3in (1.91m)
WEIGHT: 235lbs (107kg)
HOMETOWN: Wichita, Kansas
RIVALS: Jerry "The King" Lawler, The Rock

JORDAN DEVLIN

This plucky Irishman competed in Japan before joining NXT UK. From there, Jordan Devlin garnered international acclaim by winning the NXT Cruiserweight Championship.

HEIGHT: 5ft 10in (1.78m)
WEIGHT: 180lbs (82kg)
HOMETOWN: Bray, Ireland
SIGNATURE MOVE: Ireland's Call
RIVALS: Travis Banks, Angel Garza

JOSEPH CONNERS

Once considered a hot prospect at NXT UK, Joseph Conners has since fallen out of favor with the management. He's channeling his bitterness into motivation to win titles.

HEIGHT: 6ft 1in (1.85m)
WEIGHT: 196lbs (89kg)
HOMETOWN: Nottingham, England
SIGNATURE MOVE: Don't Look Down
RIVALS: Cedric Alexander, Ashton Smith

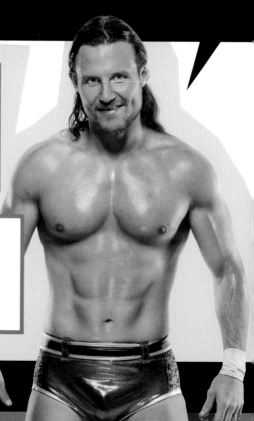

JOSIAH WILLIAMS

Hip-hop artist Josiah Williams lays down beats and rhymes that accompany the NXT Superstars to the ring. He is also an expert analyst on WWE's social-media channels.

HOMETOWN: Milwaukee, Wisconsin

JUNKYARD DOG

A Superstar beloved by the youngest members of the WWE Universe, Junkyard Dog (or JYD) often brought young fans into the ring to dance with him before or after matches.

HEIGHT: 6ft 3in (1.91m)
WEIGHT: 280lbs (127kg)
HOMETOWN: Charlotte, North Carolina
SIGNATURE MOVE: Thump Powerslam
RIVALS: Harley Race, "The Million Dollar Man" Ted DiBiase

THE KABUKI WARRIORS

Japanese Superstars Asuka and Kairi Sane make a powerful and graceful tag team. The Kabuki Warriors used their combined skills to win the WWE Women's Tag Team Titles.

SIGNATURE MOVE: The Green Mist

RIVALS: Bayley and Sasha Banks, The IIconics

KAIRI SANE

ASUKA

KACY CATANZARO

After winning a popular obstacle-course TV show, Kacy Catanzaro brought her unique in-ring style to NXT. Each time she competes, Kacy reminds the NXT Universe of her impressive talent.

HEIGHT: 5ft (1.52m)

HOMETOWN: Belleville, New Jersey

SIGNATURE MOVE: Victory Roll

RIVALS: Rhea Ripley

KAIRI SANE

Petite and powerful, Kairi Sane wows the WWE Universe with her high-flying arsenal of moves. She is a former NXT Champion and she won the WWE Women's Tag Team Titles alongside Asuka.

HEIGHT: 5ft 1in (1.55m)
HOMETOWN: Yamaguchi, Japan
SIGNATURE MOVE: Flying Elbow
RIVALS: Shayna Baszler, Alexa Bliss

KARRION KROSS

Fall and pray as Karrion Kross comes to the ring. When Kross arrived on the NXT scene, he immediately targeted outlaw Tommaso Ciampa, displaying his ruthless dominance.

HEIGHT: 6ft 4in (1.93m)
WEIGHT: 265lbs (120kg)
HOMETOWN: Las Vegas, Nevada
SIGNATURE MOVE: Exploder Suplex
RIVALS: Tommaso Ciampa

Drew McIntyre demonstrates his hunger for victory ahead of a Fatal 4-Way Match against Ricochet and Rey Mysterio at *WWE Live* in Leeds, England (November 9, 2019).

Undertaker's younger brother Kane survived a deadly fire as a child, but he came through it a dark and demonic soul. On his WWE debut in 1997, he immediately targeted his Superstar sibling.

HEIGHT: 7ft (2.13m)

WEIGHT: 323lbs (147kg)

SIGNATURE MOVE: Tombstone

RIVALS: Undertaker, Big Show

KAY LEE RAY

Kay Lee Ray joined NXT UK for one reason: to win the NXT UK Women's Championship. Her heated rivalry with Toni Storm led to a series of epic matches and Kay Lee achieved her goal.

HEIGHT: 5ft 8in (1.73m)
HOMETOWN: Glasgow, Scotland
SIGNATURE MOVE: Swanton Bomb
RIVALS: Toni Storm, Piper Niven

KAYDEN CARTER

A former college basketball standout, Kayden Carter was trained by The Dudley Boyz. With a very different in-ring style from her fellow Superstars, Kayden is one to watch in NXT.

HEIGHT: 5ft 2in (1.57m)
HOMETOWN: The Philippines
SIGNATURE MOVE: Crucifix Driver
RIVALS: Chelsea Green

KAYLA BRAXTON

Journalist Kayla Braxton brings her reporting skills to WWE, interviewing Superstars backstage and serving as the lead host on WWE's weekly morning talk show, *The Bump*.

HEIGHT: 4ft 11in (1.50m)
HOMETOWN:
Wadley, Alabama
RIVALS: The Ilconics

KEITH LEE

"Limitless" Lee has bulldozed his way through NXT. After capturing the NXT North American Title, he further proved his power by colliding with Brock Lesnar in the 2020 Men's Royal Rumble Match.

HEIGHT: 6ft 2in (1.88m)
WEIGHT: 320lbs (145kg)
HOMETOWN: Wichita Falls, Texas
SIGNATURE MOVE: Limit Breaker
RIVALS: Johnny Gargano, Damian Priest

KEN SHAMROCK

A hard-fighting Superstar, Ken Shamrock was the first to cross over from the world of mixed martial arts. He was crowned King of the Ring in 1998 and won the Intercontinental Title.

HEIGHT: 6ft 1in (1.85m)
WEIGHT: 243lbs (110kg)
HOMETOWN: Sacramento, California
SIGNATURE MOVE: Ankle Lock
RIVALS: Vader, Viscera

KENNY WILLIAMS

With a brash, arrogant attitude, Kenny Williams believes he's the star of the show—no matter what the show is. He uses his extensive aerial arsenal to combat opponents in NXT UK.

HEIGHT: 5ft 9in (1.75m)
WEIGHT: 180lbs (82kg)
HOMETOWN: Glasgow, Scotland
SIGNATURE MOVE: Satellite DDT
RIVALS: Tyler Bate, Dave Mastiff

KERRY VON ERICH

After starring in his family's sports-entertainment promotion, WCCW, "The Texas Tornado" came to WWE and made an immediate impact by winning the Intercontinental Title.

HEIGHT: 6ft 2in (1.88m)
WEIGHT: 254lbs (115kg)
HOMETOWN: Dallas, Texas
SIGNATURE MOVE: Tornado Punch
RIVALS: Mr. Perfect, Ric Flair

KEVIN OWENS

With a sour attitude and a huge chip on his shoulder, Kevin Owens is a master of hurling both insults and fists. He is a former NXT, United States, and WWE Universal Champion.

HEIGHT: 6ft (1.83m)
WEIGHT: 266lbs (121kg)
HOMETOWN: Marieville, Canada
SIGNATURE MOVE: Pop-Up Powerbomb
RIVALS: Seth Rollins, Sami Zayn

KILLIAN DAIN

Northern Irishman Killian Dain calls himself "The Beast of Belfast," and he is. He has charged through NXT and NXT UK, pummeling his opponents and proving his dominance.

HEIGHT: 6ft 4in (1.93m)
WEIGHT: 322lbs (146kg)
HOMETOWN: Belfast, Northern Ireland
SIGNATURE MOVE: DDT
RIVALS: Matt Riddle, The New Day

KING CORBIN

Always looking for a fight, King Corbin insults anyone who crosses him and backs it up in the ring. He conquered eight other Superstars to be crowned King of WWE in 2019.

HEIGHT: 6ft 8in (2.03m)
WEIGHT: 285lbs (129kg)
HOMETOWN: Kansas City, Kansas
SIGNATURE MOVE: End of Days
RIVALS: Dolph Ziggler, Sami Zayn

KOFI KINGSTON

For years, Kofi Kingston has wowed the WWE Universe with his incredible moves. His successful pursuit of the WWE Championship at *WrestleMania 35* was dubbed "Kofimania."

HEIGHT: 6ft (1.83m)
WEIGHT: 212lbs (96kg)
HOMETOWN: Ghana, West Africa
SIGNATURE MOVE: Trouble in Paradise
RIVALS: Randy Orton, The Usos

KONA REEVES

Initially trained by WWE Hall of Famer Afa of the Wild Samoans, Kona Reeves is a fun-loving Superstar who continues to grow his skills and techniques in NXT.

HEIGHT: 6ft 3in (1.91m)
WEIGHT: 225lbs (102kg)
HOMETOWN: Honolulu, Hawaii
SIGNATURE MOVE: Hawaiian Drop
RIVALS: Aleister Black

KURT ANGLE

Olympic gold-medalist Kurt Angle came to WWE and immediately dominated the competition. He won virtually every championship WWE had, earning a spot in the WWE Hall of Fame.

HEIGHT: 6ft (1.83m)
WEIGHT: 220lbs (100kg)
HOMETOWN: Pittsburgh, Pennsylvania
SIGNATURE MOVE: Angle Slam
RIVALS: Brock Lesnar, Eddie Guerrero

KUSHIDA

A mega-popular competitor in Japan and on the independent US wrestling scene, Kushida arrived in NXT to great fanfare. This fun-loving Superstar simply loves being in the ring.

HEIGHT: 5ft 9in (1.75m)
WEIGHT: 192lbs (87kg)
HOMETOWN: Tokyo, Japan
SIGNATURE MOVE: Sakuraba Lock
RIVALS: Kassius Ohno, The Brian Kendrick

KYLE O'REILLY

As a member of the Undisputed ERA, Kyle O'Reilly has helped fulfill the faction's prophecy of championship gold in NXT. He and Bobby Fish are multi-time NXT Tag Team Champions.

HEIGHT: 6ft (1.83m)
WEIGHT: 200lbs (91kg)
HOMETOWN: Vancouver, Canada
SIGNATURE MOVE: Total Elimination
RIVALS: Imperium, Street Profits

LACEY EVANS

A US Marine, a mom, and a "Sassy Southern Belle," Lacey Evans brings a level of sophistication to the WWE Women's Division. She has zero tolerance for "nasties."

HEIGHT: 5ft 8in (1.73m)
HOMETOWN: Parris Island, South Carolina
SIGNATURE MOVE: Woman's Right
RIVALS: Sasha Banks, Natalya

LANA

As a manager, Lana developed winning strategies for her charges. Her passion for winning drove her to enter the ring as a Superstar and compete for the Women's Championship.

HEIGHT: 5ft 7in (1.70m)
HOMETOWN: Moscow, Russia
SIGNATURE MOVE: Sitout Spinebuster
RIVALS: Brie Bella, Natalya

LARS SULLIVAN

A ruthless monster of a man, Lars Sullivan had a dominant run in NXT before moving onto *RAW* and *SmackDown*, where he attacked some of the biggest legends in the ring.

HEIGHT: 6ft 3in (1.91m)
WEIGHT: 330lbs (150kg)
HOMETOWN: The Rocky Mountains
SIGNATURE MOVE: Freak Accident
RIVALS: Kurt Angle, R-Truth

LEX LUGER

Former WCW Champion Lex Luger had to prove himself again when he moved to WWE. After an unsuccessful bid for the WWE Championship, he formed a tag team with the British Bulldog.

HEIGHT: 6ft 6in (1.98m)
WEIGHT: 275lbs (125kg)
HOMETOWN: Chicago, Illinois
SIGNATURE MOVE: Torture Rack
RIVALS: Yokozuna, Sting

LIGERO

By learning the Mexican lucha libre wrestling style and combining it with his traditional British grappling skills, Ligero proved he could be a contender in NXT UK.

HEIGHT: 5ft 8in (1.73m)
WEIGHT: 160lbs (73kg)
HOMETOWN: Leeds, England
SIGNATURE MOVE: The C4L
RIVALS: Pete Dunne, Ariya Daivari

LIV MORGAN

This former member of The Riott Squad faction has broken out on her own to prove she can have solo success in WWE. Liv Morgan is now focused on winning the Women's Title.

HEIGHT: 5ft 3in (1.60m)
HOMETOWN: Elmwood Park, New Jersey
SIGNATURE MOVE: Reverse Roundhouse Kick
RIVALS: Billie Kay, Peyton Royce

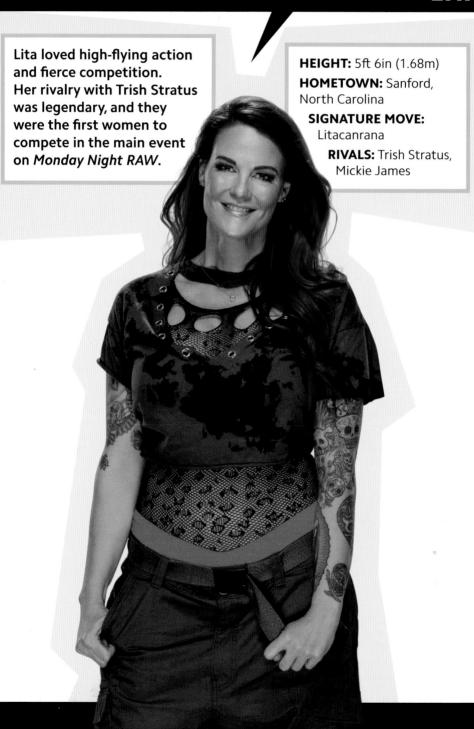

LITA

Lita loved high-flying action and fierce competition. Her rivalry with Trish Stratus was legendary, and they were the first women to compete in the main event on *Monday Night RAW*.

HEIGHT: 5ft 6in (1.68m)

HOMETOWN: Sanford, North Carolina

SIGNATURE MOVE: Litacanrana

RIVALS: Trish Stratus, Mickie James

LUCHA HOUSE PARTY

GRAN METALIK

LINCE DORADO

KALISTO

This trio of high-flying, party-loving luchadors is always excited to put on a show in the ring. They have their sights set on the *SmackDown* Tag Team Championships.

COMBINED WEIGHT: 514lbs (233kg)

SIGNATURE MOVE: Stereo Springboard Splashes

RIVALS: The Miz and John Morrison, The Forgotten Sons

MAE YOUNG

After more than 50 years in the ring, Mae Young wowed the WWE Universe by competing in her last match in her 80s. Her legend lives on in a women's tournament named for her.

HEIGHT: 5ft 4in (1.63m)

HOMETOWN: Sand Springs, Oklahoma

SIGNATURE MOVE: Bronco Buster

RIVALS: Beth Phoenix, The Dudley Boyz

"MACHO MAN" RANDY SAVAGE

"Macho Man" Randy Savage is one of the most iconic WWE Superstars ever. His physical intensity and often-erratic speeches reinforced his "Macho Madness" moniker. He was a multi-time WWE and WCW World Champion.

HEIGHT: 6ft 2in (1.88m)

WEIGHT: 237lbs (108kg)

HOMETOWN: Sarasota, Florida

SIGNATURE MOVE: Flying Elbow Drop

RIVALS: Diamond Dallas Page, The Ultimate Warrior

MAGNUM TA

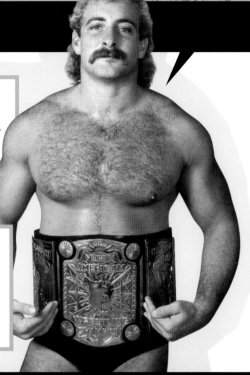

After winning the United States Championship twice in the 1980s, Magnum TA was paralyzed in a car accident. He used the same grit that he showed in the ring to learn to walk again.

HEIGHT: 6ft 1in (1.85m)
WEIGHT: 245lbs (111kg)
HOMETOWN: Virginia Beach, Virginia
SIGNATURE MOVE: Belly-to-Belly Suplex
RIVALS: Ric Flair, Tully Blanchard

MALCOLM BIVENS

Manager Malcolm Bivens is forming Bivens Enterprises—a stable of Superstars that he says will one day capture every title NXT has to offer. With tag team Indus Sher as his first signees, he just might be right.

HEIGHT: 5ft 8in (1.73m)
WEIGHT: 174lbs (79kg)
HOMETOWN: Harlem, New York
RIVALS: Matt Riddle, Robert Stone

MANDY ROSE

"God's Greatest Creation" Mandy Rose has attracted the attention of WWE Superstars like Otis and Dolph Ziggler. She is a talented competitor in the ring, punishing her opponents.

HEIGHT: 5ft 4in (1.63m)
HOMETOWN: Yorktown Heights, New York
SIGNATURE MOVE: Kiss the Rose
RIVALS: Sonya Deville, Natalya

MANSOOR

As the first Saudi Arabian-born Superstar, Mansoor feels he has a lot to prove. He has already made an impact, emerging victorious in battles against the likes of Dolph Ziggler and The Brian Kendrick.

HEIGHT: 6ft (1.83m)
WEIGHT: 190lbs (86kg)
HOMETOWN: Riyadh, Saudi Arabia
SIGNATURE MOVE: Moonsault
RIVALS: Dolph Ziggler, The Brian Kendrick

MARCEL BARTHEL

A second-generation Superstar, Marcel Barthel is a trained fighter in multiple disciplines, including grappling and boxing. He dominates NXT UK as part of the Imperium stable.

HEIGHT: 6ft 3in (1.91m)
WEIGHT: 220lbs (100kg)
HOMETOWN: Hanover, Germany
SIGNATURE MOVE: Enziguri
RIVALS: British Strong Style, Undisputed ERA

MARINA SHAFIR

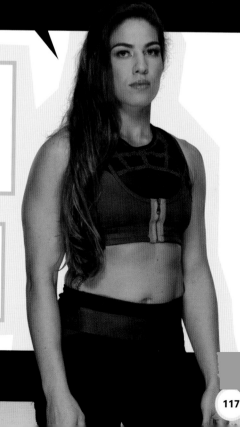

For Marina Shafir, sports entertainment is life. The former mixed martial artist is a member of the Four Horsewomen of MMA stable and is also married to fellow NXT Superstar Roderick Strong.

HEIGHT: 5ft 7in (1.70m)
HOMETOWN: Soroca, Moldova
SIGNATURE MOVE: Achilles Lock
RIVALS: Kairi Sane, Rhea Ripley

MARK ANDREWS

Mark Andrews does it all. In addition to his incredible high-flying work in the ring and winning the NXT UK Tag Team Championship, he is also the frontman of a punk-rock band.

HEIGHT: 5ft 8in (1.73m)
WEIGHT: 147lbs (67kg)
HOMETOWN: Cardiff, Wales
SIGNATURE MOVE:
Shooting Star Press
RIVALS: Grizzled Young Veterans

MARK COFFEY

Mark Coffey brings a high level of destruction to NXT UK. A former rugby player, he is like a cartoon Tasmanian devil, tearing through his opponents without remorse.

HEIGHT: 6ft 2in (1.88m)
WEIGHT: 235lbs (107kg)
HOMETOWN: Glasgow, Scotland
SIGNATURE MOVE: Crowning Glory
RIVALS: British Strong Style

MARK HENRY

Most Superstars dream of a spot in the Hall of Fame, but Mark Henry wanted to induct them into his "Hall of Pain." A former weightlifter, Henry won the World Heavyweight Title.

HEIGHT: 6ft 4in (1.93m)
WEIGHT: 360lbs (163kg)
HOMETOWN: Silsbee, Texas
SIGNATURE MOVE:
World's Strongest Slam
RIVALS: Big Show, Shawn Michaels

MARLENA

Marlena is a calculating manager who is always plotting schemes to help her charges win matches. She has also spent time as a backstage interviewer, gathering intel for her devious plans.

HEIGHT: 5ft (1.52m)
HOMETOWN: Gainesville, Florida
RIVALS: Chyna, Trish Stratus

MARYSE

A two-time WWE Divas Champion, Maryse is a vicious and determined competitor. Alongside her husband, The Miz, Maryse is the star of reality TV show *Miz & Mrs*.

HEIGHT: 5ft 8in (1.73m)
HOMETOWN: Montreal, Canada
SIGNATURE MOVE: French Kiss
RIVALS: Melina, Brie Bella

MATT RIDDLE

"The Original Bro" Matt Riddle is as chilled as they come outside the ring, but inside the ring is a different matter. The former mixed martial arts fighter is ruthless in battle.

HEIGHT: 6ft 2in (1.88m)
WEIGHT: 216lbs (98kg)
HOMETOWN: Las Vegas, Nevada
SIGNATURE MOVE: Bromission
RIVALS: Timothy Thatcher, Velveteen Dream

MAURO RANALLO

After starting out as an announcer in Stampede Wrestling in Canada, Mauro Ranallo brought his talents to NXT. A mental-health advocate, Ranallo is supportive of the NXT Superstars in and out of the ring.

HEIGHT: 5ft 9in (1.75m)
HOMETOWN: Abbotsford, Canada
SIGNATURE PHRASE: "Mamma mia!"
RIVALS: Undisputed ERA

THE MEGA POWERS

In the 1980s, no Superstars were bigger than Hulk Hogan and "Macho Man" Randy Savage. They joined forces as The Mega Powers and ruled the tag team ranks.

COMBINED WEIGHT: 539lbs (244kg)
SIGNATURE MOVE: Leg Drop/Elbow Drop Combination
RIVALS: André the Giant, "The Million Dollar Man" Ted DiBiase

"MACHO MAN" RANDY SAVAGE

HULK HOGAN

MERCEDES MARTINEZ

A fierce competitor, Mercedes Martinez honed her craft for 17 years on the independent scene. She advanced far in the Mae Young Classic tournament and is determined to be the best in NXT.

HEIGHT: 5ft 7in (1.70m)
HOMETOWN: Waterbury, Connecticut
SIGNATURE MOVE: Dragon Sleeper
RIVALS: Kacy Catanzaro, Shayna Baszler

MIA YIM

Mia Yim arrived in NXT as part of the Mae Young Classic tournament. Here to stay, the "Head Baddie in Charge" has proven a threat to every NXT Women's Champion.

HEIGHT: 5ft 7in (1.70m)
HOMETOWN: Fontana, California
SIGNATURE MOVE: Protect Ya Neck
RIVALS: Candice LeRae, Shayna Baszler

MICHAEL COLE

For more than two decades, Michael Cole has been the voice of WWE. As the lead announcer on *SmackDown*, he calls matches and interviews Superstars on the blue brand.

HEIGHT: 5ft 9in (1.75m)
WEIGHT: 169lbs (77kg)
HOMETOWN: Amenia, New York
RIVALS: Jerry "The King" Lawler, Corey Graves

MICHAEL HAYES

All the time is party time for Michael Hayes! As part of The Fabulous Freebirds, he is a multi-time tag team champion and was inducted into the WWE Hall of Fame in 2016.

HEIGHT: 6ft 4in (1.93m)
WEIGHT: 255lbs (116kg)
HOMETOWN: Atlanta, Georgia
SIGNATURE MOVE: DDT
RIVALS: The Von Erich Family

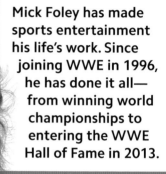

MICK FOLEY

Mick Foley has made sports entertainment his life's work. Since joining WWE in 1996, he has done it all—from winning world championships to entering the WWE Hall of Fame in 2013.

HEIGHT: 6ft 2in (1.88m)
WEIGHT: 287lbs (130kg)
HOMETOWN:
Long Island, New York
SIGNATURE MOVE:
Mandible Claw
RIVALS: Undertaker, Vader

MICKIE JAMES

Mickie James made a big impact on her 2005 debut by winning the Women's Championship. Five years and five titles later, Mickie left WWE but returned in 2017 in pursuit of more gold.

HEIGHT: 5ft 4in (1.63m)
HOMETOWN: Richmond, Virginia
SIGNATURE MOVE: Mick Kick
RIVALS: Trish Stratus, Becky Lynch

MIKE ROME

Mike Rome has found himself perfectly at home as a ring announcer in WWE. His background as a game-show host has made him a fan favorite on *RAW* and other WWE events.

HEIGHT: 6ft 2in (1.88m)
HOMETOWN: San Diego, California
RIVALS: The Singh Brothers

"THE MILLION DOLLAR MAN" TED DIBIASE

"The Million Dollar Man" Ted DiBiase used smart strategies in the ring. But if he couldn't win with his talents alone, he was known to buy victories with his money.

HEIGHT: 6ft 1in (1.85m)
WEIGHT: 260lbs (118kg)
HOMETOWN: Palm Beach, Florida
SIGNATURE MOVE: Million Dollar Dream
RIVALS: Dusty Rhodes,
Jake "The Snake" Roberts

THE MIZ AND JOHN MORRISON

These multi-time tag team champions are also Hollywood A-Listers. The Miz and John Morrison host their own talk show on WWE TV and have appeared in music videos, TV shows, and movies together.

COMBINED WEIGHT: 436lbs (198kg)
SIGNATURE MOVE: Starship Pain/ Skull-Crushing Finale combination
RIVALS: The New Day, The Usos

THE MIZ

JOHN MORRISON

THE MIZ

A former WWE Champion, The Miz has shown he can get the job done, both in the ring and on the screen. When he's not competing in *SmackDown*, he's walking the red carpet or shooting his latest movie.

HEIGHT: 6ft 2in (1.88m)
WEIGHT: 221lbs (100kg)
HOMETOWN:
Hollywood, California
SIGNATURE MOVE:
Skull-Crushing Finale
RIVALS: John Cena, Dean Ambrose

MOJO RAWLEY

Ex-football player Mojo Rawley is about as high energy as they come. After debuting in NXT, he was drafted to *SmackDown* and won the André the Giant Memorial Battle Royal at *WrestleMania 33*.

HEIGHT: 6ft 4in (1.93m)
WEIGHT: 265lbs (120kg)
HOMETOWN:
Alexandria, Virginia
SIGNATURE MOVE: Hyperdrive
RIVALS: Zack Ryder

MOLLY HOLLY

A cousin of Superstars Hardcore Holly and Crash Holly, Molly Holly forged her own path in WWE. She became the Hurricane's superhero sidekick, Mighty Molly, and later won the Women's Title.

HEIGHT: 5ft 4in (1.63m)
HOMETOWN: Forest Lake, Minnesota
SIGNATURE MOVE: Molly-Go-Round
RIVALS: Ivory, Trish Stratus

MOUSTACHE MOUNTAIN

Tough British blokes Trent Seven and Tyler Bate have a reputation for finely groomed facial hair and hard-hitting in-ring action. They use British Strong Style fighting techniques.

TRENT SEVEN

TYLER BATE

COMBINED WEIGHT: 391lbs (177kg)
SIGNATURE MOVE: Seven Stars Lariat
RIVALS: Imperium, Undisputed ERA

MR. PERFECT

Mr. Perfect, Curt Hennig, lived up to his name and proved his flawless athletic ability to the WWE Universe by winning both the Intercontinental and United States Championships.

HEIGHT: 6ft 3in (1.91m)
WEIGHT: 257lbs (117kg)
HOMETOWN: Robbinsdale, Minnesota
SIGNATURE MOVE: Perfect-Plex
RIVALS: Bret "Hit Man" Hart, Ric Flair

Kofi Kingston attempts to seal victory against Robert Roode using his Trouble in Paradise signature move at *Friday Night SmackDown* (February 28, 2020).

MR. MCMAHON

The number-one rule when dealing with the Chairman of WWE, Mr. McMahon, is: Don't cross the boss. He controls Superstars' destinies, firing them on a whim or placing them in difficult matches.

HEIGHT: 6ft 1in (1.85m)

HOMETOWN: Greenwich, Connecticut

SIGNATURE PHRASE: "You're fired!"

RIVALS: Stone Cold Steve Austin, D-Generation X

MR. T

A mega Hollywood star in the 1980s, Mr. T competed at the first two *WrestleMania* events. His boxing match against "Rowdy" Roddy Piper is still an iconic *WrestleMania* moment.

HEIGHT: 5ft 10in (1.78m)
WEIGHT: 236lbs (107kg)
HOMETOWN: Chicago, Illinois
SIGNATURE MOVE: Right Hook
RIVALS: "Rowdy" Roddy Piper, "Cowboy" Bob Orton

"MR. WONDERFUL" PAUL ORNDORFF

An iconic Superstar of the 1980s, "Mr. Wonderful" Paul Orndorff competed in many memorable matches, notably in a steel-cage match on one of the first episodes of *Saturday Night's Main Event*.

HEIGHT: 6ft (1.83m)
WEIGHT: 252lbs (114kg)
HOMETOWN: Brandon, Florida
SIGNATURE MOVE: Piledriver
RIVALS: "Rowdy" Roddy Piper, "Cowboy" Bob Orton

MURPHY

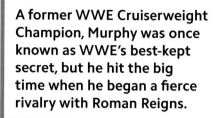

A former WWE Cruiserweight Champion, Murphy was once known as WWE's best-kept secret, but he hit the big time when he began a fierce rivalry with Roman Reigns.

HEIGHT: 5ft 11in (1.80m)
WEIGHT: 227lbs (103kg)
HOMETOWN: Melbourne, Australia
SIGNATURE MOVE: Murphy's Law
RIVALS: Shinsuke Nakamura, Kota Ibushi

MUSTAFA ALI

Former Chicago police officer Mustafa Ali came to WWE as part of the Cruiserweight Classic tournament. His high-flying approach to in-ring competition has wowed the WWE Universe.

HEIGHT: 5ft 10in (1.78m)
WEIGHT: 182lbs (83kg)
HOMETOWN: Chicago, Illinois
SIGNATURE MOVE: Inverted 450 Splash
RIVALS: Drew Gulak, Lince Dorado

NAOMI

After starting out in WWE as a dancer, Naomi transitioned to Superstar and won the *SmackDown* Women's Title. In her neon ring gear, she wants everyone to "Feel the Glow."

HEIGHT: 5ft 5in (1.65m)
HOMETOWN: Orlando, Florida
SIGNATURE MOVE: Slay-O-Mission
RIVALS: Alexa Bliss, Charlotte Flair

NATION OF DOMINATION

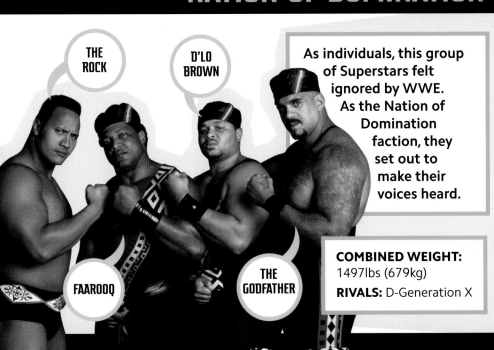

THE ROCK

D'LO BROWN

FAAROOQ

THE GODFATHER

As individuals, this group of Superstars felt ignored by WWE. As the Nation of Domination faction, they set out to make their voices heard.

COMBINED WEIGHT: 1497lbs (679kg)
RIVALS: D-Generation X

NATALYA

A third-generation WWE Superstar, Natalya is a member of the legendary Hart Family. She added the *SmackDown* Women's Championship to her family's golden legacy.

HEIGHT: 5ft 5in (1.65m)
HOMETOWN: Calgary, Canada
SIGNATURE MOVE:
Sharpshooter
RIVALS: Nikki Bella, Becky Lynch

Propelled by the power of positivity, The New Day always put smiles on people's faces, whether they're setting tag team championship records or performing energetic moves in the ring.

COMBINED WEIGHT: 702lbs (318kg)
SIGNATURE MOVE: Midnight Hour
RIVALS: The Bar

BIG E

KOFI KINGSTON

XAVIER WOODS

NEW AGE OUTLAWS

"Oh, you didn't know?" The New Age Outlaws didn't care about following the rules or respecting their opponents. Their unruly ways made them six-time WWE Tag Team Champions.

"ROAD DOGG" JESSE JAMES

BILLY GUNN

COMBINED WEIGHT: 501lbs (227kg)
SIGNATURE MOVE: Spike Piledriver
RIVALS: Mick Foley and Terry Funk, The Shield

NIA JAX

At six-feet tall, Nia Jax towers over other female Superstars in WWE. The former *RAW* Women's Champion uses her unmatched strength and agility to punish opponents.

HEIGHT: 6ft (1.83m)
HOMETOWN: San Diego, California
SIGNATURE MOVE: Leg Drop
RIVALS: Alexa Bliss, Bayley

NIGEL MCGUINNESS

Once a champion competitor around the world, Nigel McGuinness joined WWE as a commentator and brought his experienced analysis to NXT, NXT UK, and *205 Live*.

HEIGHT: 6ft 3in (1.91m)
WEIGHT: 225lbs (102kg)
HOMETOWN: London, England
RIVALS: Mauro Ranallo

NIKKI CROSS

Wild and unpredictable, Nikki Cross has carved out a place for herself on *SmackDown*. Along with her best friend, Alexa Bliss, Nikki is a two-time Women's Tag Team Champion.

HEIGHT: 5ft (1.52m)
HOMETOWN: Glasgow, Scotland
SIGNATURE MOVE: The Purge
RIVALS: Bayley, Sasha Banks

NIKOLAI VOLKOFF

A staunch opponent of the US during the 1980s, Nikolai Volkoff would sing his country's national anthem before matches. He saw success in the tag team ranks.

HEIGHT: 6ft 4in (1.93m)
WEIGHT: 313lbs (142kg)
HOMETOWN: Moscow, Russia
SIGNATURE MOVE: Bear Hug
RIVALS: Hulk Hogan, Sgt. Slaughter

NINA SAMUELS

With in-ring experience across Europe, Nina Samuels brings a devastating arsenal of moves to NXT UK. She's determined to be the star attraction for the black-and-gold brand.

HEIGHT: 5ft 7in (1.70m)
HOMETOWN: London, England
SIGNATURE MOVE: Prima Donna
RIVALS: Toni Storm, Kay Lee Ray

NOAM DAR

Born in Israel and raised in Scotland, Noam Dar represents both nations in the ring. A mat-focused competitor, he prefers submission holds to high-risk aerial maneuvers.

HEIGHT: 5ft 9in (1.75m)
WEIGHT: 178lbs (81kg)
HOMETOWN: Ayr, Scotland
SIGNATURE MOVE: Kneebar
RIVALS: Cedric Alexander

NORMAN SMILEY

He is a multi-time WCW Hardcore Champion, but Norman Smiley was terrified of hardcore matches! He wore protective sports gear and screamed as his opponents attacked.

HEIGHT: 6ft 2in (1.88m)
WEIGHT: 240lbs (109kg)
HOMETOWN: Northampton, England
SIGNATURE MOVE: The Big Wiggle
RIVALS: Finlay, Bam Bam Bigelow

Rebellious and dangerous, the nWo changed sports entertainment forever. The faction ran roughshod over WCW, resulting in a TV ratings war with WWE and the dawn of the Attitude Era.

COMBINED WEIGHT:
1129lbs (512kg)

RIVALS: The Four Horsemen, Stone Cold Steve Austin, The Rock

RAZOR RAMON

HULK HOGAN

KEVIN NASH

ONEY LORCAN

A hardworking and hard-hitting Superstar, Oney Lorcan plies his craft primarily in NXT. Claiming to feel no pain, he has powered through brutal injuries to win matches.

HEIGHT: 6ft 1in (1.85m)
WEIGHT: 190lbs (86kg)
HOMETOWN: Boston, Massachusetts
SIGNATURE MOVE: Single-Leg Boston Crab
RIVALS: Drew McIntyre, Hideo Itami

OTIS

One half of Heavy Machinery, Otis has found success in tag team and singles competition. He won the 2020 Money in the Bank Match and now plans to capture the Universal Title.

HEIGHT: 5ft 10in (1.78m)
WEIGHT: 330lbs (150kg)
HOMETOWN: Superior, Wisconsin
SIGNATURE MOVE: Compactor
RIVALS: Dolph Ziggler, King Corbin

PAIGE

Paige was the first NXT Women's Champion and won the Divas Championship on her first night in WWE. After retiring due to injury, Paige briefly became General Manager of *SmackDown*.

HEIGHT: 5ft 8in (1.73m)
HOMETOWN: Norwich, United Kingdom
SIGNATURE MOVE: Paige Turner
RIVALS: Charlotte Flair, Natalya

PAPA SHANGO

A mysterious voodoo master, Papa Shango used a mix of technical wrestling and mystical forces to defeat his opponents. His spells could make them sick or even set them on fire.

HEIGHT: 6ft 6in (1.98m)
WEIGHT: 330lbs (150kg)
HOMETOWN: Parts Unknown
SIGNATURE MOVE: Shoulder Drop
RIVALS: The Ultimate Warrior, Hulk Hogan

PAT PATTERSON

Everywhere Pat Patterson went, he made history. The first Intercontinental Champion, he also won the WWE Hardcore Championship 40 years after his 1958 debut.

HEIGHT: 6ft 1in (1.85m)
WEIGHT: 237lbs (108kg)
HOMETOWN: Montreal, Canada
SIGNATURE MOVE: Atomic Drop
RIVALS: Sgt. Slaughter, The Wild Samoans

PAUL BEARER

Spooky and smart, Paul Bearer was the longtime manager of the Undertaker. He helped to channel unseen mystical forces to give "The Deadman" an advantage in the ring.

HEIGHT: 5ft 10in (1.78m)
HOMETOWN: Death Valley, California
SIGNATURE PHRASE:
"Ohhhh yeeesssss"
RIVALS: "The Million Dollar Man" Ted DiBiase, Edge

PAUL ELLERING

As the manager of The Road Warriors, Paul Ellering guided the highly successful tag team to championships all over the world. He returned to WWE in 2016 to manage AOP in NXT.

HEIGHT: 5ft 10in (1.78m)
HOMETOWN:
Minneapolis, Minnesota
SIGNATURE PHRASE: "Beware the Legion of Doom!"
RIVALS: The Four Horsemen, Dusty Rhodes

PAUL HEYMAN

He managed in AWA and WCW, owned the original ECW, and was General Manager of *SmackDown*. But Paul Heyman is perhaps best known for leading Brock Lesnar to countless titles in WWE.

HEIGHT: 5ft 11in (1.80m)
HOMETOWN: Scarsdale, New York
SIGNATURE PHRASE: "Ladies and gentlemen, my name is Paul Heyman!"
RIVALS: Goldberg, Roman Reigns

PETE DUNNE

Pete Dunne held the NXT UK Championship for 685 days—the longest title reign in modern WWE history—and he is a former NXT Tag Team Champion with Matt Riddle.

HEIGHT: 5ft 10in (1.78m)
WEIGHT: 205lbs (93kg)
HOMETOWN: Birmingham, England
SIGNATURE MOVE: The Bitter End
RIVALS: Tyler Bate, Johnny Gargano

PIPER NIVEN

Piper Niven charged into NXT UK after competing in the Mae Young Classic tournament. She's battled several Women's Champions, determined to one day win the title herself.

HEIGHT: 5ft 8in (1.73m)
HOMETOWN: Ayrshire, Scotland
SIGNATURE MOVE: Powerslam
RIVALS: Toni Storm, Kay Lee Ray

RANDY ORTON

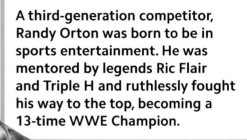

A third-generation competitor, Randy Orton was born to be in sports entertainment. He was mentored by legends Ric Flair and Triple H and ruthlessly fought his way to the top, becoming a 13-time WWE Champion.

HEIGHT: 6ft 5in (1.96m)
WEIGHT: 250lbs (113kg)
HOMETOWN: St. Louis, Missouri
SIGNATURE MOVE: RKO
RIVALS: Jinder Mahal, Bray Wyatt

RAQUEL GONZÁLES

Second-generation Superstar Raquel Gonzáles is a rough-and-tumble competitor. Since joining NXT, she has served as a bodyguard and tag team partner for Dakota Kai.

HEIGHT: 6ft (1.83m)
HOMETOWN: Rio Grande Valley, Texas
SIGNATURE MOVE: Cutter
RIVALS: Tegan Nox, Mia Yim

RAUL MENDOZA

Since entering WWE in the Cruiserweight Classic tournament, Raul Mendoza has been on a meteoric rise in NXT. He has lightning-quick moves in the ring.

HEIGHT: 5ft 7in (1.70m)
WEIGHT: 190lbs (86kg)
HOMETOWN: Córdoba, Mexico
SIGNATURE MOVE:
Shining Wizard
RIVALS: Andrade, Velveteen Dream

"RAVISHING" RICK RUDE

"Ravishing" Rick Rude knew that he had one of the most impressive physiques in WWE. That combined with his in-ring talent brought him huge success, including the Intercontinental Championship.

HEIGHT: 6ft 3in (1.91m)
WEIGHT: 252lbs (114kg)
HOMETOWN: Robbinsdale, Minnesota
SIGNATURE MOVE: Rude Awakening
RIVALS: Jake "The Snake" Roberts, The Ultimate Warrior

RAZOR RAMON

Oozing machismo, Razor Ramon was a multi-time Intercontinental Champion. When he left WWE for WCW in 1996, he created the dominant New World Order faction.

HEIGHT: 6ft 7in (2.01m)
WEIGHT: 287lbs (130kg)
HOMETOWN: Miami, Florida
SIGNATURE MOVE: Razor's Edge
RIVALS: Shawn Michaels, Stone Cold Steve Austin

REY MYSTERIO

"Booyaka! Booyaka!" A sports-entertainment legend, Rey Mysterio has competed in WWE, ECW, and WCW. His trademark masks and incredible aerial maneuvers have made him a fan favorite for more than 20 years.

HEIGHT: 5ft 6in (1.68m)
WEIGHT: 175lbs (79kg)
HOMETOWN: San Diego, California
SIGNATURE MOVE: 619
RIVALS: Seth Rollins, Randy Orton

RENEE YOUNG

A lifelong member of the WWE Universe, Renee Young joined WWE as an interviewer and commentator in NXT. In 2018, she became the first full-time female member of the *RAW* announce team.

HEIGHT: 5ft 5in (1.65m)
HOMETOWN: Toronto, Canada
RIVALS: The Miz, Maryse

RHEA RIPLEY

Calling herself "The Nightmare," Rhea Ripley is a dominant force. She is the only person to have held both the NXT and NXT UK Women's Championships.

HEIGHT: 5ft 7in (1.70m)
HOMETOWN: Adelaide, South Australia
SIGNATURE MOVE: Riptide
RIVALS: Toni Storm, Charlotte Flair

Arguably the greatest Superstar of all time, "The Nature Boy" Ric Flair is a 16-time World Champion. His career spanned four decades, and his signature call "Wooooo!" echoed around the world.

HEIGHT: 6ft 1in (1.85m)
WEIGHT: 243lbs (110kg)
HOMETOWN: Charlotte, North Carolina
SIGNATURE MOVE: Figure-Four Leg Lock
RIVALS: Sting, Ricky "The Dragon" Steamboat

RICKY "THE DRAGON" STEAMBOAT

Combining high-flying attacks with his mastery of martial arts, Ricky "The Dragon" Steamboat captured the imaginations of the WWE Universe and won several championships.

HEIGHT: 5ft 10in (1.78m)
WEIGHT: 235lbs (107kg)
HOMETOWN: Honolulu, Hawaii
SIGNATURE MOVE: Diving Crossbody
RIVALS: Ric Flair, "Macho Man" Randy Savage

RICOCHET

With his high-flying moves, Ricochet proclaims he's a real-life superhero. After winning the North American Title in NXT, Ricochet joined *RAW* and formed a tag team with Cedric Alexander.

HEIGHT: 5ft 9in (1.75m)
WEIGHT: 188lbs (85kg)
HOMETOWN:
Paducah, Kentucky
SIGNATURE MOVE: 450 Splash
RIVALS: Adam Cole, AJ Styles

RIDDICK MOSS

A college football standout, Riddick Moss transitioned from the gridiron to the wrestling ring. He then took the WWE 24/7 Championship from his friend Mojo Rawley on *RAW*.

HEIGHT: 6ft 3in (1.91m)
WEIGHT: 245lbs (111kg)
HOMETOWN: Minneapolis, Minnesota
SIGNATURE MOVE: Powerslam
RIVALS: R-Truth, Matt Riddle

RIKISHI

A Samoan giant, Rikishi often squashed his opposition in the ring. He drew on his training in Japanese sumo wrestling to win the Intercontinental and Tag Team Championships.

HEIGHT: 6ft 1in (1.85m)
WEIGHT: 425lbs (193kg)
HOMETOWN: Samoa
SIGNATURE MOVE: Rikishi Driver
RIVALS: Edge, Stone Cold Steve Austin

"ROAD DOGG" JESSE JAMES

After debuting as Jeff Jarrett's roadie, "Road Dogg" Jesse James found success as one of D-Generation X's New Age Outlaws. He won the Intercontinental, Hardcore, and Tag Team Titles.

HEIGHT: 6ft 1in (1.85m)
WEIGHT: 241lbs (109kg)
HOMETOWN: Marietta, Georgia
SIGNATURE MOVE:
Shake, Rattle, and Roll
RIVALS: Kane, Cactus Jack

ROBERT ROODE

He vowed he would usher in the most "Glorious" era in WWE's history, and Robert Roode quickly made his mark. After winning the NXT Championship, he won two more titles in WWE.

HEIGHT: 6ft (1.83m)
WEIGHT: 235lbs (107kg)
HOMETOWN: Toronto, Canada
SIGNATURE MOVE: Glorious DDT
RIVALS: Shinsuke Nakamura, Hideo Itami

ROBERT STONE

Robert Stone has one goal: to accumulate the greatest talent in NXT and conquer the brand. He has signed talented Superstars, but also made himself the target of their rivals.

HEIGHT: 5ft 11in (1.80m)
WEIGHT: 201lbs (91kg)
HOMETOWN: The Jersey Shore, New Jersey
RIVALS: Shotzi Blackheart, Rhea Ripley

ROCKY JOHNSON

Now best known as the father of The Rock, Rocky Johnson was a legendary Superstar in his own right. He became the first African American WWE Tag Team Champion in 1983.

HEIGHT: 6ft 2in (1.88m)
WEIGHT: 260lbs (118kg)
HOMETOWN: Toronto, Canada
SIGNATURE MOVE: Dropkick
RIVALS: The Wild Samoans

RODERICK STRONG

Before coming to NXT, Roderick Strong competed all over the world for 15 years. As a member of the Undisputed ERA, Strong has seen golden success.

HEIGHT: 5ft 10in (1.78m)
WEIGHT: 200lbs (91kg)
HOMETOWN: Tampa, Florida
SIGNATURE MOVE: Sick Kick
RIVALS: Imperium, Velveteen Dream

THE ROCK

The Rock's charisma and talent led him to win 10 World Titles and worldwide fame. Whether he is competing in the ring or hosting *WrestleMania*, the WWE Universe are in for a treat when they see The Rock.

HEIGHT: 6ft 5in (1.96m)
WEIGHT: 260lbs (118kg)
HOMETOWN: Miami, Florida
SIGNATURE MOVE: The People's Elbow
RIVALS: John Cena, Stone Cold Steve Austin

ROMAN REIGNS

Roman Reigns is known as "The Big Dog," and WWE is his yard. The former WWE Champion uses his incredible strength to power through to the top of WWE and to conquer life-threatening leukemia.

HEIGHT:
6ft 3in (1.91m)
WEIGHT:
265lbs (120kg)
HOMETOWN:
Pensacola, Florida
SIGNATURE MOVE:
Spear
RIVALS: Brock Lesnar, Braun Strowman

"Rowdy" Roddy Piper spoke his mind, made people angry, and fought like a wild man in the ring. He won the Intercontinental Championship late in his career and served for a time as President of WWE.

HEIGHT: 6ft 2in (1.88m)
WEIGHT: 230lbs (104kg)
HOMETOWN:
Glasgow, Scotland
SIGNATURE MOVE:
Sleeper Hold
RIVALS: Goldust, Ric Flair

"The Big Dog" Roman Reigns prepares for battle against "The Beast"—Universal Champion Brock Lesnar—at *WrestleMania 34* (April 8, 2018).

R-TRUTH

Rapping his way to the ring, this eccentric veteran Superstar gets the WWE Universe to echo his call, "What's Up?" R-Truth has won multiple titles and is a 35-time WWE 24/7 Champion.

HEIGHT: 6ft 2in (1.88m)
WEIGHT: 220lbs (100kg)
HOMETOWN:
Charlotte, North Carolina
SIGNATURE MOVE: Lie Detector
RIVALS: Goldust, The Miz

RUBY RIOTT

With a punk-rock attitude, Ruby Riott came to WWE with two goals in mind: to cause chaos and to become Women's Champion. She once led her own Riott Squad faction.

HEIGHT: 5ft 4in (1.63m)
HOMETOWN: Lafayette, Indiana
SIGNATURE MOVE: Overhead Kick
RIVALS: Asuka, Nikki Cross

SAM GRADWELL

Perpetually angry, Sam Gradwell has a ruthless fighting style that has brought him many victories in the ring and made him a big threat to the NXT UK Champion.

HEIGHT: 6ft 1in (1.85m)
WEIGHT: 212lbs (96kg)
HOMETOWN: Blackpool, England
SIGNATURE MOVE: Flying Splash
RIVALS: Pete Dunne, Tyler Bate

SAMI ZAYN

He may not be the biggest Superstar, but there's no doubt that Sami Zayn has one of the biggest hearts in WWE. Ever the underdog, Zayn puts all he has into his matches.

HEIGHT: 6ft 1in (1.85m)
WEIGHT: 220lbs (100kg)
HOMETOWN: Montreal, Canada
SIGNATURE MOVE: Helluva Kick
RIVALS: Braun Strowman, Kevin Owens

SAMOA JOE

A former NXT and United States Champion, Samoa Joe destroys opponents with his mixed martial arts-inspired offensive style. He now brings his experience to the announcer desk on *RAW*.

HEIGHT: 6ft 2in (1.88m)
WEIGHT: 282lbs (128kg)
HOMETOWN: Huntington Beach, California
SIGNATURE MOVE: Coquina Clutch
RIVALS: Seth Rollins, Brock Lesnar

SANTANA GARRETT

Rising star Santana Garrett was trained by WWE Hall of Famers Razor Ramon and Larry Zbyzsko. An experienced gymnast and grappler, she has superhero-like abilities.

HEIGHT: 5ft 5in (1.65m)
HOMETOWN: Ocala, Florida
SIGNATURE MOVE: Shining Star Press
RIVALS: Shayna Baszler, Bianca Belair

SANTOS ESCOBAR

Formerly known as the masked Superstar El Hijo del Fantasma, Santos Escobar unmasked himself and took on a new name and a bad attitude after winning the Interim NXT Cruiserweight Title.

HEIGHT: 5ft 11in (1.80m)
WEIGHT: 198lbs (90kg)
HOMETOWN: Mexico City, Mexico
SIGNATURE MOVE: Top Rope Dive
RIVALS: Gentleman Jack Gallagher

SARA AMATO

After making a name for herself in sports entertainment worldwide, Sara Amato caught the attention of WWE officials, who hired her as the assistant head coach at WWE's Performance Center.

HEIGHT: 5ft 9in (1.75m)
HOMETOWN: Martinez, California
SIGNATURE MOVE: Fallaway Slam
RIVALS: Mia Yim

SASHA BANKS

Sasha Banks is a scrappy Superstar with a lifelong passion for WWE. She calls herself "The Boss," and with good reason—she's become a multi-time WWE Women's Champion.

HEIGHT: 5ft 5in (1.65m)
HOMETOWN: Boston, Massachusetts
SIGNATURE MOVE: Bank Statement
RIVALS: Charlotte Flair, Bayley

SAXON HUXLEY

As his nickname suggests, "The Muscle Cat" Saxon Huxley is agile, precise, and powerful in the ring. He was trained by WWE legend Lance Storm and Superstar The Brian Kendrick.

HEIGHT: 6ft 3in (1.91m)
WEIGHT: 220lbs (100kg)
HOMETOWN: Hartlepool, England
SIGNATURE MOVE: Shattered Illusions
RIVALS: Trent Seven, Sam Gradwell

SCARLETT

Intimidating and dangerous, Scarlett calls on the NXT Universe to "fall and pray" as she guides evil Superstar Karrion Kross to the ring ahead of his matches.

HEIGHT: 5ft 5in (1.65m)
HOMETOWN: Chicago, Illinois
SIGNATURE MOVE: Suplex
RIVALS: Tommaso Ciampa

SETH ROLLINS

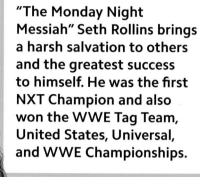

"The Monday Night Messiah" Seth Rollins brings a harsh salvation to others and the greatest success to himself. He was the first NXT Champion and also won the WWE Tag Team, United States, Universal, and WWE Championships.

HEIGHT: 6ft 1in (1.85m)
WEIGHT: 217lbs (98kg)
HOMETOWN:
Davenport, Iowa
SIGNATURE MOVE:
Pedigree
RIVALS: Triple H,
Roman Reigns

SGT. SLAUGHTER

A former US Marine drill sergeant, Sgt. Slaughter brought a brutal level of aggression to the ring. Following his retirement, Sgt. Slaughter became Commissioner of WWE.

HEIGHT: 6ft 4in (1.93m)
WEIGHT: 310lbs (141kg)
HOMETOWN:
Parris Island, South Carolina
SIGNATURE MOVE: Cobra Clutch
RIVALS: Iron Sheik, Pat Patterson

SHANE MCMAHON

Being the WWE Chairman's son can be challenging, but Shane McMahon has asserted his authority in the family business. He is a former WWE European and Hardcore Champion.

HEIGHT: 6ft 2in (1.88m)
WEIGHT: 230lbs (104kg)
HOMETOWN: New York City, New York
SIGNATURE MOVE: Coast-to-Coast
RIVALS: Kurt Angle, AJ Styles

SHAWN MICHAELS

"The Heartbreak Kid" Shawn Michaels began his WWE career as a baby-faced member of tag team The Rockers. He went on to become the most celebrated and decorated Superstar of all time.

HEIGHT: 6ft 1in (1.85m)
WEIGHT: 225lbs (102kg)
HOMETOWN:
San Antonio, Texas
SIGNATURE MOVE:
Sweet Chin Music
RIVALS: Undertaker,
Bret "Hit Man" Hart

SHANE THORNE

After competing in Japan and Australia, Shane Thorne caught the attention of WWE Hall of Famer Harley Race. He has since made his name in hard-hitting matches on *RAW* and *SmackDown*.

HEIGHT: 6ft 2in (1.88m)
WEIGHT: 225lbs (102kg)
HOMETOWN: Perth, Australia
SIGNATURE MOVE: Black Swan Splash
RIVALS: Street Profits, Johnny Gargano

SHAYNA BASZLER

Mixed martial artist Shayna Baszler came to WWE in the Mae Young Classic, dominating the tournament before becoming a two-time NXT Women's Champion.

HEIGHT: 5ft 7in (1.70m)
HOMETOWN: Sioux Falls, South Dakota
SIGNATURE MOVE: Kirifuda Clutch
RIVALS: Becky Lynch, Kairi Sane

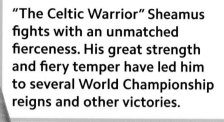

SHEAMUS

"The Celtic Warrior" Sheamus fights with an unmatched fierceness. His great strength and fiery temper have led him to several World Championship reigns and other victories.

HEIGHT: 6ft 4in (1.93m)
WEIGHT: 267lbs (121kg)
HOMETOWN: Dublin, Ireland
SIGNATURE MOVE: Brogue Kick
RIVALS: Cesaro, Daniel Bryan

SHELTON BENJAMIN

Shelton Benjamin originally joined WWE as part of Kurt Angle's Team Angle tag team. After breaking out on his own, he won the Intercontinental Championship and other titles.

HEIGHT: 6ft 2in (1.88m)
WEIGHT: 248lbs (112kg)
HOMETOWN: Orangeburg, South Carolina
SIGNATURE MOVE: Paydirt
RIVALS: Shorty G, Carlito

SHERRI MARTEL

"Sensational" Sherri Martel was a successful competitor in WWE and the AWA before managing the likes of "Macho Man" Randy Savage, Ric Flair, and Harlem Heat.

HEIGHT: 5ft 7in (1.70m)
HOMETOWN: New Orleans, Louisiana
SIGNATURE MOVE: Loaded Purse
RIVALS: Elizabeth, Luna Vachon

SHINSUKE NAKAMURA

After mastering the hard-hitting strikes and kicks of Japanese Strong Style, Shinsuke Nakamura brought his skills to WWE and quickly won numerous championships.

HEIGHT: 6ft 2in (1.88m)
WEIGHT: 229lbs (104kg)
HOMETOWN: Kyoto, Japan
SIGNATURE MOVE: Kinshasa Knee Strike
RIVALS: Dolph Ziggler, Samoa Joe

SHORTY G

Having competed in amateur wrestling at the 2012 Summer Olympic Games, Shorty G understands the technical skills needed for in-ring competition better than most Superstars.

HEIGHT: 5ft 8in (1.73m)
WEIGHT: 202lbs (92kg)
HOMETOWN: Minneapolis, Minnesota
SIGNATURE MOVE: Chaos Theory
RIVALS: Kevin Owens, Rusev

SHOTZI BLACKHEART

Shotzi Blackheart's devil-may-care attitude and high-flying arsenal amazed fans all over the world before she joined NXT. She entered the 2020 Women's Royal Rumble Match driving a tank.

HEIGHT: 5ft 6in (1.68m)
HOMETOWN: Oakland, California
SIGNATURE MOVE: Diving Senton
RIVALS: Shayna Baszler, Candice LeRae

SID SCALA

Originally an in-ring competitor in NXT UK, Sid Scala has traded his ring gear for a suit as the Assistant General Manager on the brand. He is a no-nonsense boss who won't be intimidated.

HEIGHT: 5ft 6in (1.68m)
WEIGHT: 185lbs (84kg)
HOMETOWN: London, England
SIGNATURE MOVE: Bionic Elbow
RIVALS: Imperium

THE SINGH BROTHERS

Although they came to WWE as individual competitors, The Singh Brothers, Sunil and Samir, have joined forces and become a powerful pair in the tag team ranks.

COMBINED WEIGHT:
303lbs (137kg)
SIGNATURE MOVE:
Double Superkick
RIVALS: Randy Orton, AOP

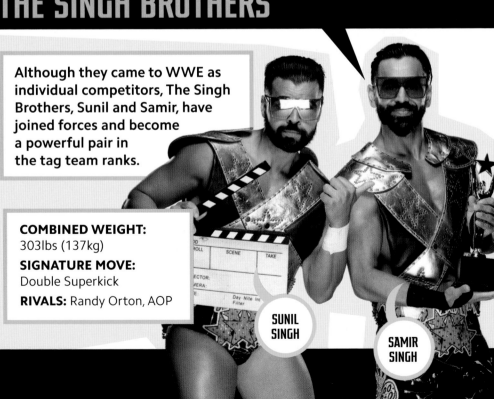

SUNIL SINGH

SAMIR SINGH

SONYA DEVILLE

With her motto "Put your hair up and square up," Sonya Deville is always looking for a fight. A proud member of the LGBTQ+ community, she brings her experience as a mixed martial artist into WWE.

HEIGHT: 5ft 7in (1.70m)
HOMETOWN: Shamong, New Jersey
SIGNATURE MOVE: Square Up Kick
RIVALS: Mandy Rose, Alexa Bliss

STREET PROFITS

The Street Profits have lit up the WWE Universe on *RAW*. The former NXT and *RAW* Tag Team Champions are an exciting duo who excel in anything they undertake.

COMBINED WEIGHT: 492lbs (223kg)
SIGNATURE MOVES: Frog Splash, Powerslam
RIVALS: The Viking Raiders, Andrade and Angel Garza

ANGELO DAWKINS

MONTEZ FORD

STEPHANIE MCMAHON

As the daughter of WWE Chairman Vince McMahon and wife to WWE Chief Operations Officer Triple H, Stephanie McMahon has amassed incredible power over the WWE Superstars. She demonstrates her ruthlessness at every opportunity.

HEIGHT:
5ft 9in (1.75m)
HOMETOWN:
Greenwich, Connecticut
RIVALS: Shane McMahon, Brie Bella

STING

Sting joined WWE as the capstone of his incredible 30-year career. The dark, brooding Superstar protected WCW from the invasion of the nWo and moved to WWE to stop Triple H's abuses of power.

HEIGHT: 6ft 2in (1.88m)
WEIGHT: 250lbs (113kg)
HOMETOWN: Venice Beach, California
SIGNATURE MOVE: Scorpion Deathlock
RIVALS: Triple H, Ric Flair

STONE COLD STEVE AUSTIN

Stone Cold Steve Austin is arguably the toughest WWE Superstar ever. A strong brawler with a rebellious nature, he fights against authority, earning him the unwavering support of the WWE Universe.

HEIGHT: 6ft 2in (1.88m)
WEIGHT: 252lbs (114kg)
HOMETOWN: Victoria, Texas
SIGNATURE MOVE: Stone Cold Stunner
RIVALS: The Rock, Bret "Hit Man" Hart

"SUPERSTAR" BILLY GRAHAM

Dressed in tie-dye and feather boas and boasting about his talents, "Superstar" Billy Graham was flashy, but he backed up his threats when he won the WWE Championship.

HEIGHT: 6ft 4in (1.93m)
WEIGHT: 275lbs (125kg)
HOMETOWN: Paradise Valley, Arizona
SIGNATURE MOVE: Bear Hug
RIVALS: Bruno Sammartino, Bob Backlund

SYCHO SID

Sycho Sid was a dominant force in WWE in the 1990s. A giant in the ring, he used his great strength and power to capture the WWE and WCW Championships.

HEIGHT: 6ft 9in (2.05m)
WEIGHT: 317lbs (144kg)
HOMETOWN: West Memphis, Arkansas
SIGNATURE MOVE: Powerbomb
RIVALS: Undertaker, Shawn Michaels

TAMINA

A second-generation Superstar, Tamina debuted with her cousins, The Usos. She's been a bodyguard, a manager, and a tag team partner. Next, she plans to be Women's Champion.

HEIGHT: 5ft 9in (1.75m)
HOMETOWN: The Pacific Islands
SIGNATURE MOVE: Superfly Splash
RIVALS: Naomi, Nikki Bella

TATANKA

Tatanka proudly represented his people, the Lumbee Native American tribe, as a fierce Superstar. He prepared for every match by performing a Lumbee war dance.

HEIGHT: 6ft 2in (1.88m)
WEIGHT: 285lbs (129kg)
HOMETOWN: Pembroke, North Carolina
SIGNATURE MOVE: Indian Death Drop
RIVALS: Lex Luger, IRS

TATSUMI FUJINAMI

A technical wizard in Japan since the 1970s, Tatsumi Fujinami made history by holding the prestigious IWGP Heavyweight and NWA World Heavyweight Championships simultaneously.

HEIGHT: 6ft (1.83m)
WEIGHT: 227lbs (103kg)
HOMETOWN: Kunisaki, Japan
SIGNATURE MOVE: Dragon Backbreaker
RIVALS: Ric Flair, Big Van Vader

TEGAN NOX

Tegan Nox is a passionate performer. After successive knee injuries put her out of action for nearly two years, she regained her strength and returned to action in NXT.

HEIGHT: 5ft 6in (1.68m)
HOMETOWN: Welsh Valleys, Wales
SIGNATURE MOVE: Shiniest Wizard
RIVALS: Dakota Kai, Candice LeRae

TERRY TAYLOR

A technical marvel in the ring, Terry Taylor competed in WWE, WCW, and sports-entertainment promotions all over the world. He is currently a coach at the WWE Performance Center.

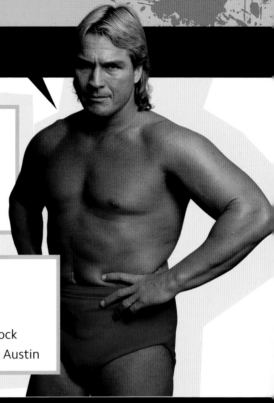

HEIGHT: 6ft 1in (1.85m)
WEIGHT: 224lbs (102kg)
HOMETOWN: Vero Beach, Florida
SIGNATURE MOVE: Figure-Four Leglock
RIVALS: Mr. Perfect, Stone Cold Steve Austin

TIMOTHY THATCHER

If his cracked teeth aren't evidence enough of his toughness, Timothy Thatcher is happy to prove it in the ring. He made his name as a competitor in Europe before joining NXT.

HEIGHT: 6ft 3in (1.91m)
WEIGHT: 228lbs (103kg)
HOMETOWN: Sacramento, California
SIGNATURE MOVE: Fujiwara Armbar
RIVALS: Matt Riddle, Undisputed ERA

TITUS O'NEIL

No one in WWE lives life with as much drive and passion as Titus O'Neil. He burst onto the WWE scene as one half of the Prime Time Players tag team and later won the 24/7 Title.

HEIGHT: 6ft 6in (1.98m)
WEIGHT: 270lbs (122kg)
HOMETOWN: Live Oak, Florida
SIGNATURE MOVE: Clash of the Titus
RIVALS: The New Day, Big Show

TOM PHILLIPS

Originally a backstage interviewer, Tom Phillips took over the lead announcer duties on *RAW* in 2020, calling the action ringside with unmatched expertise and professionalism.

HEIGHT: 6ft (1.83m)
HOMETOWN: Philadelphia, Pennsylvania
SIGNATURE PHRASE: "Welcome to *RAW*!"
RIVALS: Corey Graves

TOMMASO CIAMPA

Don't turn your back on Tommaso Ciampa or he'll betray you to get what he wants. His vicious streak and impressive technical skills led him to win the NXT Championship.

HEIGHT: 5ft 11in (1.80m)
WEIGHT: 201lbs (91kg)
HOMETOWN: Milwaukee, Wisconsin
SIGNATURE MOVE: Armbar
RIVALS: Johnny Gargano, The Revival

TONI STORM

With her punk-rock attitude and love for competition, Toni Storm has literally taken NXT UK by storm. Her intense rivalries with Rhea Ripley and Kay Lee Ray have led to legendary matches on the brand.

HEIGHT: 5ft 5in (1.65m)
HOMETOWN: Gold Coast, Australia
SIGNATURE MOVE: Storm Zero
RIVALS: Rhea Ripley, Kay Lee Ray

TONY NESE

It takes a lot of confidence to call yourself "The Premier Athlete," and Tony Nese has it. Since coming to WWE in the Cruiserweight Classic tournament, he has used his varied moves to win matches.

HEIGHT: 5ft 11in (1.80m)
WEIGHT: 196lbs (90kg)
HOMETOWN: Long Island, New York
SIGNATURE MOVE: 450 Splash
RIVALS: TJP, Rich Swann

TRENT SEVEN

He may appear to be a well-groomed, gentlemanly sort, but don't be fooled. Beneath Trent Seven's charming exterior is a hard-as-nails aggressor who strives for greatness.

HEIGHT: 6ft 1in (1.85m)
WEIGHT: 216lbs (98kg)
HOMETOWN: Wolverhampton, England
SIGNATURE MOVE: Seven Stars Lariat
RIVALS: Imperium, Undisputed ERA

TRIPLE H

For 25 years, Triple H has been one of the most dominant Superstars in WWE. The 14-time World Champion is a strategic genius in the ring, knowing exactly how to attack his opponents physically and mentally.

HEIGHT: 6ft 4in (1.93m)
WEIGHT: 255lbs (116kg)
HOMETOWN: Greenwich, Connecticut
SIGNATURE MOVE: Pedigree
RIVALS: Undertaker, Seth Rollins

TRISH STRATUS

After beginning her career as a manager, Trish Stratus fell in love with in-ring competition. She became a seven-time WWE Women's Champion and one of the best Superstars in WWE history.

HEIGHT: 5ft 5in (1.65m)
HOMETOWN:
Toronto, Canada
SIGNATURE MOVE:
Stratusfaction
RIVALS: Lita, Mickie James

TUGBOAT

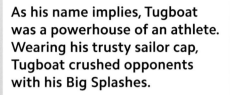

As his name implies, Tugboat was a powerhouse of an athlete. Wearing his trusty sailor cap, Tugboat crushed opponents with his Big Splashes.

HEIGHT: 6ft 3in (1.91m)
WEIGHT: 383lbs (174kg)
HOMETOWN: Lakeland, Florida
SIGNATURE MOVE: Big Splash
RIVALS: Earthquake, Dino Bravo

TYLER BATE

A technical wizard in the ring, Tyler Bate was crowned the inaugural NXT UK Champion. He has beaten the best in NXT UK and now seeks tag team glory alongside Trent Seven as Moustache Mountain.

HEIGHT: 5ft 7in (1.70m)
WEIGHT: 175lbs (79kg)
HOMETOWN: Dudley, England
SIGNATURE MOVE: Tyler Driver
RIVALS: Pete Dunne, Grizzled Young Veterans

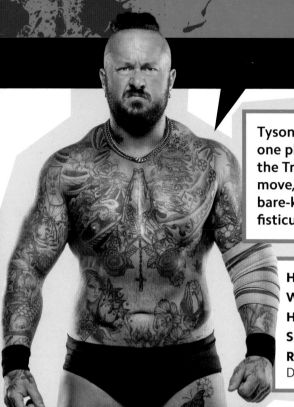

TYSON T-BONE

Tyson T-Bone never likes to stay in one place for too long. "The King of the Travelers" is always on the move, looking for a fight. This bare-knuckle brawler prefers fisticuffs to grappling.

HEIGHT: 6ft (1.83m)
WEIGHT: 245lbs (111kg)
HOMETOWN: Malvern, England
SIGNATURE MOVE: Gypsy's Kiss
RIVALS: Moustache Mountain, Dave Mastiff

UMAGA

"The Samoan Bulldozer" Umaga devastated opponents and wreaked havoc throughout WWE. After becoming the Intercontinental Champion, he served as the McMahon family's bodyguard.

HEIGHT: 6ft 4in (1.93m)
WEIGHT: 350lbs (159kg)
HOMETOWN: Samoa
SIGNATURE MOVE: Samoan Spike
RIVALS: John Cena, Triple H

THE ULTIMATE WARRIOR

The Ultimate Warrior was known for his fast-paced, hard-hitting in-ring style. The face-painted Superstar captivated the imaginations of a generation, teaching his "Little Warriors" to believe in the power of dreams.

HEIGHT: 6ft 2in (1.88m)
WEIGHT: 280lbs (127kg)
HOMETOWN: Parts Unknown
SIGNATURE MOVE: Gorilla Press Slam
RIVALS: "Macho Man" Randy Savage, Undertaker

"The Boss" Sasha Banks shows WWE Women's Tag Team Champion Nikki Cross who's in charge at *RAW* (September 23, 2019).

For 30 years, the Undertaker has inspired awe and fear in Superstars and the WWE Universe. With abilities that seem supernatural, the Undertaker has laid the biggest names in WWE history to rest in his matches.

HEIGHT: 6ft 10in (2.08m)
WEIGHT: 309lbs (140kg)
HOMETOWN: Death Valley
SIGNATURE MOVE: Tombstone
RIVALS: Shawn Michaels, Brock Lesnar

THE USOS

Second-generation Superstars Jimmy and Jey Uso were trained by their father Rikishi. For years, The Usos were a happy, fun-loving duo, but adopting a more aggressive attitude brought them even more championship gold.

COMBINED WEIGHT: 479lbs (217kg)

HOMETOWN: San Francisco, California

SIGNATURE MOVE: Double Samoan Splash

RIVALS: The New Day, American Alpha

JIMMY USO

JEY USO

UNDISPUTED ERA

If you face one member of the Undisputed ERA, you face them all. They are the most dominant force in NXT. At one point, they held every one of NXT's championships, fulfilling their "golden prophecy."

COMBINED WEIGHT: 807lbs (366kg)

SIGNATURE MOVE: Total Elimination

RIVALS: Imperium, Street Profits

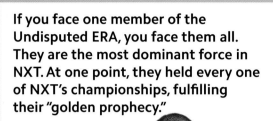

ADAM COLE

KYLE O'REILLY

BOBBY FISH

RODERICK STRONG

VADER

What time is it? It's Vader time! Known as "The Mastodon," Vader was a giant who flew through the air like a cruiserweight. He was a WCW World Heavyweight Champion.

HEIGHT: 6ft 5in (1.96m)

WEIGHT: 450lbs (204kg)

HOMETOWN: The Rocky Mountains

SIGNATURE MOVE: Vaderbomb

RIVALS: Sting, Mick Foley

VANESSA BORNE

A former dancer and cheerleader for professional football teams, Vanessa Borne changed course for WWE. Trained by legends Rikishi and Gangrel, Vanessa is an up and comer in NXT.

HEIGHT: 5ft 4in (1.63m)
HOMETOWN: Scottsdale, Arizona
SIGNATURE MOVE:
Handspring Splash
RIVALS: Xia Li

VELVETEEN DREAM

Flamboyant and manipulative, Velveteen Dream is a master of mind games. His machinations have earned him both the North American Championship and the wrath of his many rivals.

HEIGHT: 6ft 2in (1.88m)
WEIGHT: 225lbs (102kg)
HOMETOWN: Capitol Hill, Washington, D.C.
SIGNATURE MOVE: Purple Rainmaker
RIVALS: Adam Cole, Aleister Black

VIKING RAIDERS

The Viking Raiders live their lives in the style of their warrior ancestors. Clad in horned helmets, the former NXT and *RAW* Tag Team Champions conquer the proverbial land wherever they go.

COMBINED WEIGHT: 552lbs (250kg)
SIGNATURE MOVE: The Viking Experience
RIVALS: Street Profits, Seth Rollins and Murphy

ERIK

IVAR

VISCERA

Viscera rose to prominence as a member of the Undertaker's Ministry of Darkness stable. Once freed from it, he turned into the "World's Largest Love Machine."

HEIGHT: 6ft 9in (2.05m)
WEIGHT: 487lbs (221kg)
HOMETOWN: Harlem, New York
SIGNATURE MOVE: Viscera Driver
RIVALS: Undertaker, Mark Henry

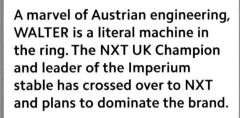

WALTER

A marvel of Austrian engineering, WALTER is a literal machine in the ring. The NXT UK Champion and leader of the Imperium stable has crossed over to NXT and plans to dominate the brand.

HEIGHT: 6ft 4in (1.93m)
WEIGHT: 310lbs (141kg)
HOMETOWN: Vienna, Austria
SIGNATURE MOVE: Powerbomb
RIVALS: Moustache Mountain, Gallus

THE WARLORD

The Warlord was one of WWE's strongest competitors in the 1990s. With his unbreakable submission hold, he destroyed his adversaries in both the tag team and singles divisions.

HEIGHT: 6ft 5in (1.96m)
WEIGHT: 323lbs (147kg)
HOMETOWN: Parts Unknown
SIGNATURE MOVE: Full Nelson
RIVALS: British Bulldog, The Bushwhackers

WENDI RICHTER

A two-time WWE Women's Champion, Wendi Richter helped grow WWE into a worldwide phenomenon in the 1980s. A fierce fighter, her matches were always exciting.

HEIGHT: 5ft 8in (1.73m)
HOMETOWN: Dallas, Texas
SIGNATURE MOVE: Sitout DDT
RIVALS: Fabulous Moolah, Leilani Kai

WILD BOAR

An unhinged and dangerous competitor with unsettling black eyes, Wild Boar tears through his opponents. Since coming to NXT UK, he has proven to be a true animal.

HEIGHT: 5ft 6in (1.68m)
WEIGHT: 204lbs (93kg)
HOMETOWN: Blaina, Wales
SIGNATURE MOVE: Facebuster
RIVALS: Ligero, Dave Mastiff

THE WILD SAMOANS

With their unpredictable in-ring style, brothers Afa and Sika won three WWE tag team championships in the 1970s and 1980s. Following their retirement in 1988, The Wild Samoans trained and managed up-and-coming Superstars.

COMBINED WEIGHT: 645lbs (293kg)
HOMETOWN: Samoa
SIGNATURE MOVE: Samoan Drop
RIVALS: Bob Backlund, Rocky Johnson

SIKA

AFA

WILLIAM REGAL

As a competitor, William Regal was difficult to defeat. When he retired, he became the Commissioner of WWE and then General Manager of NXT, where he's not afraid to physically enforce the rules.

HEIGHT: 6ft 3in (1.91m)
WEIGHT: 243lbs (110kg)
HOMETOWN: Blackpool, England
SIGNATURE MOVE: Regal Stretch
RIVALS: Adam Cole, Kofi Kingston

WOLFGANG

A tough brawler, Wolfgang likes to fight no matter where it is. Alongside the Coffey Brothers, Wolfgang is a member of the dominant Gallus faction. Together, they have battled the best in NXT UK.

HEIGHT: 6ft 3in (1.91m)
WEIGHT: 266lbs (121kg)
HOMETOWN: Glasgow, Scotland
SIGNATURE MOVE: Spear
RIVALS: British Strong Style

XAVIER WOODS

Xavier Woods' belief in the power of positivity has made him a multi-time tag team champion with The New Day. Outside the ring, Woods runs his popular video-game channel, UpUpDownDown.

HEIGHT: 5ft 11in (1.80m)
WEIGHT: 205lbs (93kg)
HOMETOWN: Atlanta, Georgia
SIGNATURE MOVE: Midnight Hour
RIVALS: The Usos, Sheamus

XIA BROOKSIDE

A self-described "firecracker," Xia Brookside is a tough competitor who can go blow for blow with the best of them. She is the daughter of NXT UK head coach Robbie Brookside.

HEIGHT: 5ft 3in (1.60m)
HOMETOWN:
Liverpool, England
SIGNATURE MOVE:
Brooksy Bomb
RIVALS: Jinny, Kay Lee Ray

XIA LI

The first Chinese woman ever to compete in a WWE ring, Xia Li has impressed the NXT Universe. After debuting in the Mae Young Classic tournament, Xia has battled her way to the top of NXT.

HEIGHT: 5ft 3in (1.60m)
HOMETOWN: Chongqing, China
SIGNATURE MOVE: Tornado Kick
RIVALS: Aliyah, Chelsea Green

X-PAC

X-Pac saw incredible success in his 20-year career. A former member of the nWo and D-Generation X factions, he won numerous titles, including the European and Cruiserweight Championships.

HEIGHT: 6ft 1in (1.85m)
WEIGHT: 212lbs (96kg)
HOMETOWN: Minneapolis, Minnesota
SIGNATURE MOVE: X-Factor
RIVALS: Chris Jericho, Ric Flair

YOKOZUNA

Yokozuna came to WWE as a successful sumo wrestler. He used his insurmountable weight advantage to plow through WWE's Superstars, winning the 1993 Royal Rumble Match and two WWE Titles.

HEIGHT: 6ft 4in (1.93m)
WEIGHT: 589lbs (267kg)
HOMETOWN: The Land of the Rising Sun
SIGNATURE MOVE: Banzai Drop
RIVALS: Bret "Hit Man" Hart, Undertaker

ZELINA VEGA

A talented in-ring competitor, Zelina Vega's best skills are found outside the ring as a manager. Her experience as a Superstar enables her to physically interfere in her charges' matches.

HEIGHT: 5ft (1.52m)
HOMETOWN: Queens, New York
SIGNATURE MOVE: Moonsault
RIVALS: Bianca Belair, Candice LeRae

Project Editor Pamela Afram **Senior Designer** Nathan Martin
Senior Pre-Production Producer Marc Staples **Senior Producer** Louise Minihane
Managing Editor Sarah Harland **Managing Art Editor** Vicky Short
Art Director Lisa Lanzarini **Publisher** Julie Ferris **Publishing Director** Mark Searle

Packaged for DK by Plum Jam
Editor Hannah Dolan **Designer** Guy Harvey

Global Publishing Manager Steve Pantaleo **Vice President, Interactive Products** Ed Kiang
Vice President, Consumer Products Sylvia Lee **Senior Vice President, Consumer Products** Sarah Cummins
Vice President—Photography Bradley Smith **Photo department** Josh Tottenham, Frank Vitucci, Georgiana
Dallas, Jamie Nelson, Melissa Halladay **Senior Vice President, Assistant General Counsel—Intellectual
Property** Creative Director John Jones **Project Manager** Brent Mitchell

First American Edition, 2021
Published in the United States by DK Publishing
1450 Broadway, Suite 801, New York, New York 10018

Page design copyright ©2021 Dorling Kindersley Limited
DK, a Division of Penguin Random House LLC
21 22 23 24 25 10 9 8 7 6 5 4 3 2 1
001–321757–Mar/2021

A CIP catalog record for this book is available
from the Library of Congress.

ISBN 978-0-7440-2774-7

DK books are available at special discounts when purchased in bulk for sales promotions, premiums,
fund-raising, or educational use. For details, contact: DK Publishing Special Markets,
1450 Broadway, Suite 801, New York, New York 10018
SpecialSales@dk.com

Printed and bound in China

For the curious

www.dk.com
www.wwe.com

MIX
Paper from
responsible sources
FSC™ C018179

This book is made from Forest Stewardship
Council™ certified paper—one small step
in DK's commitment to a sustainable future.
For more information go to www.dk.com/
our-green-pledge